IT'S TIME TO CLEAN THE BASEMENT AGAIN

Bon Voyage!

Dennis J. DeWitt

It's Time to Clean the Basement Again
Holland, Michigan, USA

ISBN 978-1-257-71216-8
LCCN

Printed in the United States of America.

Preface

This book was written from the experiences of being a parent, a teacher, a school social worker and a pastor on a spiritual journey.

I grew up in Muskegon Heights, Michigan in an intact famil with two brothers. I was the middle child. I regularly wei with my parents to church at Covenant Reformed Church, ar with Aunt Ruth Anderson to the Church of God (Andersc Indiana). At sixteen I began working at Carl's grocery sto After two years at Muskegon Community College I tra ferred to Hope College in Holland Michigan.

In the fall of 1962 I married Janna South, my high sc sweetheart. I then finished my college career in June 1963 In September 1963 I began my career as a Spanish Teacl the West Ottawa Public Schools. In 1970 Jan died of I cancer. I was a single parent, and a widower with four children. Mark was seven, Jim five, Karin three and Kristen eight months old. Two weeks after the funeral I teaching again. After several unsuccessful sitters I was hire Grace, the wife of a seminary student from Canadε

Sometime later I met and married Mary Kuiper who h children. Combined, we had seven children under eiɡ of age.

It's Time to Clean the Basement Again

Seeing what children experience in death and divorce, I decided to pursue a degree in social work to help children in schools. That career began in 1973 and continued for 20 years.

Attending the First annual Men's Conference at the Crystal Cathedral in 1992 I heard a distinct call to ministry.

I entered Western Theological Seminary in 1993. Graduating in May of 1996, I was called to Community Church of Douglas where I continue in ministry.

As Mary and I were raising a family it seemed that we would often use the expression "it's time to clean the basement again". If a child went to camp we would go to the basement and find the sleeping bag, and whatever was needed for camp. Children reentering from college would bring things home and we would find room in the basement for them. The basement of our house held many stories. All of us have things stored in "the basement". This book is a collection of writings from experiences in teaching, social work and ministry from a parent's perspective.

I believe very strongly in legacy. Thus some of my writings include what could be considered "memoirs."

Cleaning the basement

The title of this book reflects changes that happened in our home. When we built a bedroom in the basement, we had to do considerable cleaning and organizing because our storage space was now about 9' x 12'. This included a workbench and minimal storage for out of season clothing. Moving nine

people into the house also meant providing space for nine bicycles in the garage.

Along with the physical changes to the house, in our family they were psychological changes. Blending families means some give-and-take. What once was a boy being the oldest child, now becomes a girl being the oldest. Loss issues surface in the blending process. In our family we felt it a healthy strategy to share feelings with a trusted person. Sometimes it would be an aunt or uncle or grandparent. On occasion seeing a minister or a licensed consulting psychologist was helpful for bringing out the issues that needed processing. Rather than calling it counseling, I prefer to use the word "coach".

Dedication

To my wife Mary and our blended family.

Blessings to all of you, children and grandchildren.

Acknowledgements

I've often heard that everyone has a book inside them and this book began as a seed 20 years ago. I discussed it with a psychologist friend Dr. David Register. He asked what my motivation was. My response was, "To help others on the journey of life, especially someone in a blended family". He was especially pleased that my motivation was not money. Subsequently, I went on a two day silent retreat and outlined the contents of my book. Chapter 16 is a result of that particular opportunity.

In Holland, Michigan there is an organization called the Hope Academy Senior Professionals (HASP). Within HASP, I joined a writing group called "memoirs "led by Mary Heideman. Every other week I would write something to present to this group and found encouragement to continue writing.

As I would write, I would send copies to Nancy Nauta. She was very encouraging to me to continue writing. Barbara Mezeske, a Hope College English teacher did a superb job of editing.

The manuscript was given to several people to read and make comments. I am grateful for the work of Wayne Hamilton, Darrel Schregardus, Janeen Fowler and John DeJong. Their comments were especially helpful.

My wife, Mary, has been more than patient with me as I've gotten up early in the morning to write or to edit.

Contents

PEOPLE

APPENDIX
ANDERSON FAMILY HISTORY

Beginning

1

GROWING UP IN
MUSKEGON HEIGHTS, MICHIGAN

In the 1930's Marvin and Martha DeWitt were married and paid $1,250 for their house at 1537 Sanford Street in Muskegon Heights, Michigan. That was seven dollars down and five dollars a month paid to Pete Holmes, a longtime friend and insurance man. After a number of years went by 1537 Sandford was legally changed to 3036 Sanford Street to reduce confusion between Muskegon and Muskegon Heights addresses.

Our home consisted of a small kitchen, single stall garage, one bathroom with a claw foot tub, a 9' x 12' bedroom and a 12'x12' living room. When their first son Larry was born, my parents extended the living room six feet and put a12' x 12' bedroom on the front. There was a basement underneath the original house that contained a coal room, a coal burning furnace, a workbench and a place to hang laundry to dry in the winter. The garage had room for a wringer washer and laundry tubs with hot and cold water hoses.

In the summer, clothes were hung outside on a folding umbrella clothes rack. Mother had a broom with her when she hung up the clothing, because Blue Jays would swoop down and attack her. As the saying went "Monday was wash day, Tuesday ironing." Mother used an iron with an ironing board set up in the kitchen. She also had a mangle iron in the basement for doing flat items like sheets and pillowcases. In the winter clothing hung up in the basement sometimes took more than a day to dry. Metal frames were put inside blue jeans to give them a crease and to avoid some ironing. I remember when I was in junior high school I had one pair of pants and two shirts because I was growing so fast. That meant that they were washed often.

Sunday dinner was always a beef roast, with the round bone cut. My mother always got the tenderloin because she had "store teeth." Along with the roast we would have mashed potatoes with gravy, and most often applesauce and cooked carrots. Sometimes the carrots and potatoes would go in the same roasting pan with a beef. Many Sundays my mother would put the carrots to cook on top of a gas stove in an aluminum pan. When the carrots smelled like they were done, she would get up from reading the Sunday paper and put dinner on the table. Often the carrots burned the bottom of the pan and if it couldn't be cleaned sufficiently, a new one was purchased. If the evidence is true about aluminum and Alzheimer's, we should be good candidates.

Monday always meant not only laundry day, but leftovers. The beef from Sunday was ground and made into hash with onions and ketchup. Often we had potato pancakes from leftover mashed potatoes. Because our dad was up so early and ate breakfast while he was delivering milk, we often had pancakes or oatmeal for supper on Tuesdays. Wednesdays we had my Grandmother DeWitt over for dinner, so a larger meal was prepared. On Thursday our mother went to what she called "a hen party." Many times it was her church circle, or neighbors from the farm. That meant that we had tuna noodle casserole: cream of mushroom soup, canned tuna fish and canned peas all put together and baked with potato chips on top (corn flakes for variety). Friday night was often hot dogs and chips.

One of our monthly meals would be Chef Boyardee pizza because the pizza sauce came in a can that could be used to fix the tailpipe on the Nash Ambassador car. It just fit in place with two hose clamps. I have a vivid memory of my dad under the car fixing the exhaust pipe.

Our home on the corner of Sanford and Rotterdam always seemed to be a safe place to grow up. A two block walk to Glendale school for the first five years was convenient. Sixth grade meant a one mile walk to Roosevelt school. In 1952 we got our first television set and I would come home for lunch and watch "Love of Life" and "Search for Tomorrow" each being 15 minutes long allowing just enough time to eat lunch and finish my time with Joanne Tate and Stu Irwin. This was also the year that Eisenhower became President and Elizabeth

13

was crowned Queen of England. Howdy Doody came on at three o'clock in the afternoon and, of course, we remember Uncle Milty sponsored by Texaco.

With junior high school came new opportunities. Being part of the orchestra I remember trying out for a new chair playing the violin. The other person and I finished the piece we were to play. Mr. Golumbeck, the orchestra director asked what the title of the piece was. I'm sure "The Russian Sailors Dance." was unrecognizable to him. That year as I was growing, I grew into the cello. Previously I had been using the violin my dad used when he was in high school. A talent show was organized when I was in the ninth grade. I played string bass, my friend Fred played drums, and another friend Barry played piano. We really jammed.

Our yard was always very well cared for. We used a reel type lawnmower, and collected the grass with the catcher behind. We would mow the lawn in two directions. Because Uncle Sam made sprinklers, we always used his, and often there were trips to his home to repair them. We had a number of perennials including hostas all the way around the house. My mother called them "green leafy plants." We later transplanted some of the hostas to our house on Natchez. The other flowers were iris. Mother called them "flags." When I was in junior high I made a small wooden wheelbarrow to plant flowers in. We planted some beautiful petunias in it and, placed it in the front yard. Soon after, someone stole it. I still remember the design of that wheelbarrow, and feel I could duplicate it.

The expression "cleanliness is next to godliness" was one of the expressions heard and practiced in our home along with.

"You don't go to a funeral in a dirty car" or "You don't go to church in a dirty car," "Saturday is the day to polish shoes to get ready for Sunday." "Did you wash your elbows clean?" "Never bring a car home on empty."

Celebrations

New Year's Day was always spent at Uncle Sam and Aunt Emma's house. We would arrive in time to watch the Rose Bowl Parade, of course on black-and-white television. We were able to be creative, imagining what the floats looked like in color. Between the parade and the football game my dad and Uncle Red played cribbage, while some of us played Caroms on the board that Sam put permanently on top of a card table, and made the surface highly polished. My mother, Aunt Emma and Aunt Leona worked in the kitchen and mostly talked about church activities. Emma and Leona sang in the choir. Dinner was always ham, mashed potatoes and specially made gravy. Sam always took many pictures of family events.

Birthdays were celebrated with pickle and bologna sandwiches. The pickle and bologna were ground together. Because our kitchen cupboards and countertops had limited space, my mother screwed the grinder onto a small wooden chair. (That chair is now in our basement. You can still see the marks where the grinder was put on top of the chair).

Church

Growing up in Muskegon Heights, we went to Covenant Reformed Church. Because my dad was a milk man, he only had every seventh day off. One week his day off would be Monday, next week Tuesday etc.

15

It's Time to Clean the Basement Again

John Post a friend of the family drove us to church every Sunday, and because he was in the adult Sunday school class we also stayed for Sunday school. I cannot recall my mother going to church with us on those Sundays. When we went together to church it usually was Sunday evening worship. Our minister The Rev. James Stegeman was tall and had a very loud voice. He was the minister who baptized me in 1941. My recollection was that we stood for the "long prayer". Many times that prayer would last 10 to 15 minutes or longer.

My cousin Dave and I made confession of faith on the same evening at Covenant Reformed Church. It was on a Maundy Thursday. After church we went to see the Disney movie *The Shaggy Dog*.

Many Sunday nights we went to the Muskegon Heights Church of God with Aunt Ruth Anderson. Her parents, grandpa and grandma Anderson were members of the Lutheran Church in Norway. They went to a tent meeting and were "saved", and thus when the minister said that my grandmother should not be "bound up or adorned", (he said it was scriptural), my grandmother took off her wedding ring and girdle and put them in the collection plate for missions. My grandfather gave up smoking, drinking and gambling. As a "hybrid", I had training in the Reformed Church and in the Church of God.

Now back to night church and the Church of God. Very vigorous singing opened up the worship service. Most Sunday night's Aunt Ruth was the song leader. We sang the old gospel favorites. Then we would come to the song "it was on a Monday that someone touched me, or it was on a Tuesday that somebody touched me, and must've been the hand of the Lord." When this was sung you were expected to stand on the

day you were "touched". As a member of Covenant Reformed Church I never felt "touched". I never knew when to
stand up. The rule was, if you didn't know which day you
were saved, and then everyone would stand up on "Sunday". I
became much acquainted with the concept of being "saved"
because at the end of the service, those who were in front as
"the repentant saved" were then prayed for and anointed with
oil. The sick were also anointed with oil. Services at Covenant
Church were somewhat predictable, whereas services in the
Church of God had many surprises and a lot of spontaneity.
Frequently I'd hear "Amen, hallelujah, praise the Lord and
yes, Lord". Brother Shroeder was a longtime minister of the
church. Along came the Revs.Raab. Brother Raab preached at
one service, and his wife, Sister Raab preached the other service. She was a far better preacher. He sounded and looked
like Alfred Hitchcock, big stomach and all. I would say that
most of my spiritual influence came from Aunt Ruth. She died
about a year before I began at Community Church, but she
knew I was in seminary and she said that she always knew I
would be a minister.

Vacations

Typically our family went to Big Blue Lake north of Muskegon. We stayed in a cottage and took along the Chris-Craft kit boat that my dad and uncles built one winter. My dad owned a four horsepower Mercury motor that he put on the back of the boat to be able to take a gentle ride on the lake, or go fishing. Fishing days were long because we were told not to talk, for fear we would not catch fish. Dad was also an extremely quiet man who didn't talk much. If we caught fish, Dad cleaned them, Mother fried them, and when dinner was over Dad lit up a stogie to get the fish smell out of the cottage. The fish were small, had many bones, and were a lot of work to eat.

One year, one of the factories in Muskegon paid all of its employees in two dollar bills or silver dollars. Therefore many people paid their milk bill with two dollar bills or silver dollars. Mother and Dad saved what they could from this to pay for a vacation. We went up north across the Mackinaw Bridge shortly after it opened. We then went to Tahquamenon Falls and around Lake Superior. We stayed in small cabins; carrying most of our own food using a cooler made from an old milk box and a propane gas stove to heat food. This necessitated traveling light with little luggage.

Recreation
I remember dad going hunting and fishing with his brother Red, most often hunting on Uncle Ben's farm, just north of Grand Haven on Taft Road. We raised our dogs as hunting dogs. One year my dad had some extra money saved and bought a purebred beagle named Rotterdam Rock. Rocky slept in a pen outside except on frigid nights. He was a stocky dog, bred to catch rabbits.

Dad had a tent for ice fishing which he used on Mona Lake and Muskegon Lake. Sometimes he would go to Stearn's Bayou on Spring Lake. There were a lot of memories on Spring Lake because an uncle of Dad's drowned there one winter.

Music

"When in Our Music God Is Glorified" is a theme of growing up on Sanford Street.

We always had a decent record player/stereo. Dad listened to "Sons of the Pioneers" frequently on 78 RPM records. On Wednesday nights Grandma DeWitt came for dinner and to listen to "Ted Mack and The Original Amateur Hour."
My brother Larry bought a monaural record player and I remember listening to the classics on that player. These records were 33 1/3 RPM.

Singing in choir at age 16 under the leadership of Emma Bulthouse, I learned that the music for the church should be scriptural. I learned some fine music. I also learned that if one week you sing a number with a loud bang, the next week you sing something quieter. People do not like to have loud music every Sunday.

In junior high school I graduated from violin to the cello. In high school I continued with cello and also played bass drum for football games because I was big enough to carry the drum and could keep a beat.

It's Time to Clean the Basement Again

One Sunday night I played a cello solo for the offertory at Covenant Church. The piece was the overture to the *Messiah* with organ accompaniment.

Along with singing in choir, I sang in a mixed Quartet at various churches in town. I also directed a high school girl's choir at church and occasionally we sang for Sunday morning services. I remember doing "Lift Thine Eyes" by Felix Mendelssohn. We also did a Cantata for three-part women's voices.

While in high school I was invited to sing in a men's audition choir. I did that for one year while in college.

I Remember Mama

The television show "I Remember Mama", was a regular in our household. Sitting in front of a black-and-white TV set meant there was no conversation, but only attention to the television program. Being of Norwegian descent, this became a model of what I thought a family should look like, warm, caring and engaged in interaction.

Growing up in Muskegon Heights I felt very safe. This was a time when you could ride your bike or roller state on the sidewalk. I was good friends with Carl Burgess next door. He went on to be an Assembly of God minister. Next to the Burgess family were the Sims. He had only one leg and she barked at us if we touched a blade of grass on her sidewalk. Their neighbors were Greek Orthodox. No one in our neighborhood appeared to be very active in the church other than The Burgesses. I still wonder where Carl Burgess is. I was told he served the church in Battle Creek, Michigan. He moved away from The Heights when I was in sixth grade. During times of missionary furlough, the Burgesses Aunt and

20

Uncle came with their son Stanley. We would often hear ringing in the neighborhood Sta-a-a-nle-ey. This family lived in India as missionaries and came to the Heights about every seven years. I ran into Stanley 20 years ago at a conference in Chicago. He seems to have grown up.

Once a year, people would line up all around the block to get their free chickens at Meister Feed Store. There was a limit on the number of chicks that they could get. The chicks were free with the understanding that these people would buy their feed from Meister's. The Meisters were good German folk, and as I became friends with Eric their son, I also enjoyed their cooking. Many Saturdays were spent in the kitchen helping Mrs. Meister wax the kitchen floor with paste wax. We would take turns pulling each other around the floor on a rug, giving the tile a high gloss.

During the first 15 years of my life, our neighborhood was all white families. One home two doors from us had a "for sale" sign. Mr. Meister came to our house to ask for money to buy that house, so that he could rent it out to a white family. That money was not a loan, but a gift. When my father died we tried to get that money back, but found out it was nonrefundable as a gift. To my knowledge there were no black families living in the block I grew up on until 1968.

The things that influenced me most as I was growing up were probably:
- There was considerable structure and predictability in our home.
- We had a sense of community in our neighborhood with all the neighbors being friendly to each other.

21

It's Time to Clean the Basement Again

- Family was very important. Aunt Ruth was the family member most influential, being like a spiritual grand-parent.

2

GOING TO WORK WITH DAD

Getting up at 2:30 in the morning, on the first day of summer vacation, is not what most 10-year-olds plan on doing. My father woke me up, I had a quick breakfast, got dressed and we were out the door by 2:45 AM. There was a 20 minute drive in the new black Nash Ambassador to Highland Park Dairy in downtown Muskegon. We parked in the parking lot and went inside to get Divco truck number 10. (If mother needed the car, she would take dad to work, and pick him up, as there was only one family car.)

Dad drove the truck up to the cooler, where he had placed his order for the day the afternoon before. He knew how to load a truck the right way, putting the large bottles in first, then the quart bottles, followed by butter, cottage cheese, margarine and eggs.

Once the truck was loaded with ice packs on top of the cases, it was off to the Doo Drop Inn with a large load of milk, butter and cottage cheese. Dad was always the first to stop at the Doo Drop Inn with their order, and on two occasions caught someone trying to rob the restaurant. Once this delivery was made, it was time to go out for breakfast. My dad would have seven cups of coffee before 9 AM.

It's Time to Clean the Basement Again

The sun was just beginning to come up in the east; the sky was pink and blue with a few gray clouds. The noisy street sweepers were moving along the curb, garbage men were working on their route, and we were a part of the awakening day.

Going door to door delivering milk early in the morning, was not a social engagement. Milk was put in the milk box on the step, or in a special door on the side of the house. Many orders were the same for the Monday, Wednesday, and Friday run; or for the Tuesday, Thursday and Saturday delivery.

This was all part of the early "Greening of America" because only reusable glass milk bottles were used. Glass bottles were returned to the dairy, washed and refilled with a cardboard stopper and a paper cover. (I can remember bringing tubes of cardboard stoppers to school when I was in the third grade to be used as math counters).

The nine o'clock stop for coffee was at Nibble a Scrib Nib, a local counter stool -- burger place. They were one of the customers who wanted delivery in the midmorning.

Dad's route was a mixture of homes and businesses. All of the business owners and route people were quite friendly to dad.

Dad was active as a union steward with the Teamsters.

There were two magazines in our magazine rack, the *Church Herald* and the *Teamsters* magazine. I grew up thinking that Dave Beck and Jimmy Hoffa were wonderful men, as presidents of the Teamsters.

There was always an abundance of milk, cottage cheese and whipping cream at our house. We also grew up with real butter. I remember whipping cream being a topic of frequent discussion. My dad always said to keep the bowl and beaters chilled in the refrigerator before you try to make whipping cream. My mother would forget, fail, and be chastised by Dad. Aerosol "Ready whip" was not invented by that time.

We arrived at Bill Stearns restaurant just in time for lunch. Many times the cook would prepare a sandwich for Dad that he would take home and share with the whole family. The stack of meat was enough to make five sandwiches. Because I was along, we ate lunch at the restaurant.

During the day, Dad was very outgoing, friendly to the customers, and engaged well in "small talk." One to one with me, he was more reserved. When we were at home, there was very little conversation. My dad worked hard, and provided a decent living for us.

3

THE GROCERY BOY

Some days I think it would be fun to be able to go back to carrying out groceries for a living. I've often talked about going to a local grocery store to apply for a job. My wife says I'm too old for the young guys, too young for the old guys.

For six years I worked at Carl's Grocery Store in Muskegon Heights, Michigan. I started when I was 16 years old and continued until I was a junior in college. My older brother worked at Carl's. He did a good job and so when it was time for me to apply, and I was accepted quite easily.

Carl's Grocery Store was on the corner of Broadway and Peck Streets, next to Parsons Department Store. At one time there was a hardware store between Carl's and Parsons: my grandfather Harry DeWitt's store called "the Buckley Hardware Store". Grandpa DeWitt died when my dad was two years old. The large safe with Grampa's name on it from the hardware store was in Carl's Grocery Store. My mother and Aunt Ruth both worked at Parsons Department Store. This meant that there was considerable history within these two buildings. My mother's family bought groceries at Carl's, the DeWitt family bought groceries there also. The three block walk to work was a short one.

I have several recollections about working at the grocery store, many of them unrelated to each other. Thus I'm going to share some bullet points:

- Every New Year's Eve was spent taking inventory. We would close the store early, have dinner at a local "greasy spoon", and then go back to the store and count every can and box. We also had to weigh all the produce, meat and bulk dry goods. This of course was before the age of computers, so everything was hand-written and tallied by hand. Most often this task lasted until late in the evening, so never was there energy or time for a New Year's Eve party. We were paid for the time as "regular time". There was no such thing as overtime for us in those days.

- Being tall, I was often asked to take things off from the top shelf. People saved the grocery slips and were given "premiums" for reaching a certain level of money spent. This was prior to the store giving out "S&H Green Stamps". Most of the premiums were on the top shelves of the store. Such items as a picnic basket, Thermos bottle, sheets, towels, toasters and coffee pots were among the premiums. Not wanting to take the space from regular grocery products, these premiums were often in hard to reach places. When I heard my name called, I usually knew what they were looking for my height and my ability to reach "the treasures". The checkout ladies, Sylvia Hice being short, and Esther Musk being older appreciated my willingness to get the products for them.

- We had two checkout lanes and after working in the store for some time, I was trained as a cashier. Many people charged their groceries and paid for them monthly. The customer would make payments on their account at the office where large amounts of money were kept in the safe. The cash registers were not 10 key. If an item was $1. 35 you had to punch the three numbers into the cash register and hit the key that totaled. If the electricity went out we had a hand crank to work the cash register. Very quickly I learned how to make change. At the end of the day I was responsible for making sure that the cash drawer receipts matched the tally on the cash register.

- Bagging groceries was a challenge. There was no choice of paper or plastic. All bags were paper. We learned of course to put the heavy items on the bottom and the lighter one's on top. Boxes were also a choice for packaging groceries as a way of using the boxes that brought in the stock.

- As a bagger we were told to put free samples in the grocery bag. I remember putting laundry detergent in a separate bag so that the produce would not smell of soap. Cartons of three cigarettes were often given to the customer. I remember giving out "Camels", "Winstons" and "Lucky Strikes". Little did we know then that we were encouraging an addiction to nicotine and the resulting health hazards.

- Because the grocery store was a block from the city parking lot, most groceries had to be carried to cars a city block away. If the customer was lucky to find a parking place on the street it was a shorter walk.

- Occasionally a customer would give it a $.10 or $.25 tip. I especially found it interesting that people who drove expensive cars rarely tipped. People with Chevys or Fords would more frequently tip.

- One of my regular customers drove a DeSoto with wide white walls. The white walls would always be clean. She told me she would wash the tires and not the entire car because if you have clean white walls your car looks clean. To this day I always look at tires to see if they are clean. She also regularly gave me a tip.

- Starting pay at Carl's was $.75 an hour. If you worked at Meijer's Thrifty Acres you were paid $.85 an hour, but you had to pay union dues of five cents an hour. Carl's was within walking distance from home. Working at Thrifty Acres would have meant needing transportation.

- One day, one of the carryout boys said that the boss wanted us to wear white shirts and ties to carryout groceries, beginning on Saturday. Workers at Meijer's were required to wear white shirts and ties. I went out and bought a new white shirt and tie and showed up for work on Saturday all dressed up. I was the only one wearing a white shirt and tie. I was gullible, easily influenced and trusting what others said. I had not checked with the boss to see if this was a new rule, most likely because I was in awe of the boss's position and didn't want to bother him.

- There was certain stability with this staff at the grocery store. Long-term employees could be counted on to be at work on time and perform their duties as assigned. It came as a shock to me when Bill Fellows resigned as manager at Carl's to be able to own his own store in Nunica, Michigan. I figured he would be there forever. I thought the store would be there forever. Silly me. As stated in the paragraph above, I was rather naïve and my world was very small. When Bill Fellows left, my world changed. I was given more responsibilities for management. Most frequently I set up and took down the produce racks. Every morning produce was taken from the cooler and put in refrigerated display shelves. At night the rack was taken down and put in the cooler. Especially on weekends everything was dismantled and given a fresh start on Monday morning. I especially remember cutting apart blocks of dates, sealing cellophane around each package, weighing them and putting the price on. As I was in the later years of working in the store, the boss offered me the position of manager, and gave me an alternative of hundred dollars towards tuition if I continued in college. I took the hundred dollars and entered my junior year at Hope College.

- That store continued to decline over the years and by 1970 Lawrence Carl closed the doors and currently is boarded up and empty. I still wonder if the DeWitt safe is still there. It was very large and heavy. I do have a three drawer wooden file cabinet that belonged to my Grandpa DeWitt. That is a treasure that I cherish.

4

KEEPING SCORE

One Sunday Neal Boelkins said to my dad "Marv, would you and Martha like to go to Finger's Restaurant after church?" "Yes, we would" answered my dad. Neal then took my parents to his house, poured a glass of wine, set out some cheese and crackers and called Fingers Restaurant for a reservation. They drove to Grand Rapids, had a very fine meal, went for a ride, and then dropped my parents off at their home.

The following Sunday my dad asked Neal if he would like to go out for dinner. The answer was yes. My parents then brought Neal and Lillian to their home, poured a glass of wine, set out some cheese and crackers, and called Fingers Restaurant for a reservation. They again had a tasty dinner, and my parents took the Boelkins for a ride after dinner and then brought them home. *The score was even.*

When I was alone with four children and met Mary with three children we decided to get married and chose my house to accommodate the large family. A space in the basement was made into a bedroom for three boys. That space needed to be rewired with wall switch outlets around the room, and over-head lights with a switch. My dad's friend Roy Olson volunteered to do the electric work. He was 82 years old and a long-time friend of the family. He came to the house with rubber soled shoes and worked with some of the wires live. He would say "this one's hot," "this one's not." He got everything working well and I was very appreciative. I went to write him a check and he refused to take it, wanting to give this labor as a gift. This really bothered my dad because he wanted to keep the score even. I wrote a thank you note to Roy and he replied that that was payment in full. It still didn't satisfy my father who regularly would ask if I had paid Roy the money.

It is not possible to keep all scores even. Sometimes we have to be good receivers and accept a person's gifts. Sometimes we do what is called "pay forward."

In 1974 my father died shoveling snow off the roof on a cold February afternoon. Our minister, the Rev. Robert Hoeksema came to our home immediately to watch our seven children so that we could go and be with my mother at such a traumatic time.
I asked how I could repay him and he said "You can help someone else someday, in a similar situation." I have heard those words repeated in my head frequently, as I have been ministering to families in need, or experiencing trauma or loss.

Everyone has a variety of gifts. Not all people can paint pictures, sing a solo, or do electrical work. Trying to keep things even creates considerable stress. In our family we used The Family Meeting to discuss policy. During a one hour meeting everyone had one vote and only the motions with complete agreement would pass. This became an equalizer and gave power to the individual. Yet, when it came time for chores, not all tasks require the same amount of time. If you try to keep score on such issues, it is a losing game.

A New Chapter In Life

5

"I HAD A DREAM LAST NIGHT THAT YOU MET SOMEONE AND GOT MARRIED AGAIN." MOVING ON

These words were spoken by my mother-in-law just two weeks after her daughter, my wife Jan, died of breast cancer at the age of 28. Mom and I were doing dishes together on Sunday noon and I was a young widower with four small children. In no way did I feel I would be dating again, and certainly not thinking of remarriage at this time.

Not only were the words of my mother-in-law important, the source was also significant. When a parent loses a child, that parent is in a key position for a future relationship with the new in-law. As parents, we provide guidance for our children, yet how often do we think of giving permission for them to explore a new venture, take a risk, or say it is acceptable to move into a new stage in the grieving process. This relationship extends to the surviving spouse, the grandchildren and possible step grandchildren.

This gracious woman not only recently had buried a daughter who died at a young age, but she many years previously, lost an eight-year-old son to diphtheria, a disease feared at the time but now almost never heard of. Given these losses of young children, she could have been angry with God, and not been able to reach out and think of another person. Yet these words of permission allowed me, several months later to ask someone for a date. This permission was important. When the time came to introduce a new person to the family, I knew that the stage had been set for acceptance and welcome from Jan's parents.

We do not always recognize the working of the Holy Spirit at the time something significant is happening to us. When we look back, we see many examples of this movement in our lives. This was one. Jan's mother's dream could well be ex-plained as the working of the Holy Spirit. When we see situ-ations we cannot explain away otherwise, we need to listen to the power of the Holy Spirit in our lives, especially those times when life takes an unplanned direction... This might be just one occasion where the Spirit has nudged us into a new path.

One might ask,
"What is the difference between giving permission and being an enabler?"

PERMISSION -encouraging a person to follow his or her vision, giving support, communicating love, opening new doors to new ventures, and encouraging a person to take risks. The task of encouraging another means we have to move out of our own narcissistic self, and think of the needs of another person. We are called to move away from our selfish expecta-tions. Prayer is one way of providing support and moving out of our own world, into the life of another, invoking the Holy Spirit to intervene in their lives.

In December of 1972 we celebrated Christmas with my parents and their dog, in their tiny living room. It was very confining to seven small children... As I was ready to leave, my dad put his hand on my shoulder and told me I was doing a good job raising my family. This was perhaps the first time he'd used positive touch in my lifetime; touch was usually related to discipline, often quite punitive. This was very freeing to me, giving me permission to relax around him, knowing I had received a blessing. Three months later, he died suddenly of a heart attack, while shoveling snow from a flat roof. My two brothers never received this kind of affirmation and blessing. Their grieving took on a different perspective.

Several traditions bring examples of rituals of permission, rites of passage or blessing:

The Jewish tradition celebrates a bar mitzvah for a young person to" come of age" in the faith.

The Mexican tradition of the Quinceniera is celebrated with a worship service followed by food and dancing. A young girl of the family celebrates her 15th birthday, a rite of passage that dates back to the indigenous culture and employs symbols that become important as families help a child become part of the adult community. In ancient traditions, boys came apart from the family to be part of the Warriors and the tribe. Young girls also needed rituals to become part of the adult community. In the church ceremony various symbolic gifts are given to a young girl. The following are a few:

A **white dress** is a symbol of purity.

The **ring** as a symbol of tying a young girl's responsibility to the community

A **coin** signifies that the girl is under the care of a saint and walks with protection.

The **last doll** is given announcing that the girl is now an adult.

Many times a **crown** is placed on her head, helping her know that her life will be victorious.

Parents and grandparents say words of blessing and love. In return the girl shows appreciation for the many gifts she has received from her parents, siblings, grandparents and friends of the family.

Within the Mexican tradition fiestas are times to celebrate with the best food, music, dancing, and clothing. This makes the event very special. The church gives the blessing of the religious community and the fiesta celebrates life.

In the Protestant tradition, confirmation is the time of learning the doctrines of the church and in making a profession of faith. Dr. Robert Hoeksema, senior pastor of Third Reformed Church in Holland, Michigan, suggested we write a letter to our children in a confirmation class. We were to share our feelings, recalling how we brought our children to the church for baptism. We were to explain how each child got his or her name. It was then suggested that we would share any words of blessing we would want to write. Having two children in the class, Mary and I each chose our own birth child for this assignment.

As I reflect on the experience, I was able to tell my son that he was named after both of his grandfathers in a unique way, that he was a wanted child and that his birth mother would have been very pleased that he had reached this stage in his spiritual development. The letters were given to the children at a retreat and when they came home, the responses they gave were very meaningful. We need to be able to express our love for children in many ways. Putting words on paper provides for a lasting record.

ENABLING: is defined as helping someone to make an event possible. It often means taking on too much of the work that needs to be done by the other person. In recent years this term has taken on a negative meaning especially in use as "enabling "another person with addictive behavior. The addictive behavior is covering up the pain of lost relationships or painful life experiences.

As parents we are in a position of being role models for our children. If we take ownership of tasks they need to work out, we handicap them. The parent might prevent a child from accomplishing a very important developmental task.

Proverbs 19:19 reads "do not rescue the angry man, for you will have to do it again." We need to work ourselves out of a job as parents. Wanting to reduce the pain a child suffers is a natural tendency, yet it is most important for children to learn their lessons. If we intervene in a child's learning stage, we have a tendency to handicap that child as he or she will not have learned the proper lesson.

A lesson learned at a young age is with a person for life. It has been said "the youngest age is the cheapest lesson." Lessons learned in later life bring with them guilt for having made numerous mistakes in previous years. Often also there are financial costs that are greater even than also the possibility of estrangement among family or friendship relationships. Isn't it much better to learn skills at a young age and have the freedom to explore new avenues later in life? The consequences of our decisions grow larger as we age. A five-year-old learning the lessons of shoplifting brings with it a reprimand. A 15-year-old stealing from the store begins to build a juvenile court record. A 25-year-old stealing something reaps jail time, restitution and public shame.

The youngest age is the cheapest lesson

6

BLENDING FAMILIES

In my work as a pastor I often say "the days are long, the years are short". When working with parents of young children I would hear about the energy it takes to raise a family and how the days can become very long. Visiting people in nursing homes also presents situations where the days drag on and yet the years roll by fast. For Mary and me personally, small groups have really helped us in raising a family and maintaining healthy relationships.

I first learned about Koinonia in a church bulletin announcement in September of 1970 when I was a single parent with four small children. I had been part of a couples group with my wife Jan, and now was told I was not a couple and did not belong to that group anymore. A gathering was held in the Fellowship hall of the church on a Sunday evening. About 75 people were milling about and groups were then formed. The group I joined included a couple where the man was a college math teacher, a business man and his wife, who was an elementary principal and his wife an elementary teacher, a woman who served as a seminary librarian and part time organist, a college music education teacher and an invited guest – a woman college student about my age. We decided to meet in someone's home and discuss articles from the church denominational magazine *The Church Herald*. We agreed to meet in October. That meeting was interesting, so we decided to meet in November. Meeting in the home of the Seminary Librarian, I began a conversation with the college student. I discovered that she (Mary) was a single parent also. We talked about babysitters and wills for parents of young children.

Early in December I was invited to go Christmas caroling with some friends from church. I called the hostess to see if she would invite this same woman to join the carolers. She did, Mary came along and we had a nice conversation. Our December Koinonia meeting was held after a church Christmas program.

Apart from the Koinonia meetings, I called Mary the day after Christmas to go sledding with the children. We did that and went to her house afterwards for hot chocolate. This began a series of dates with all seven children.

One night I would prepare supper, and Mary and her three children would join us in my three bedroom ranch on the north side of Holland. Because many of the children were in school, we ate early and then often we would continue our conversation by phone after Mary and her children had gone home. When Mary prepared dinner I would pack up my four children in my two door sedan and we would go to Mary's house. Mark and Jim were in first and third grades and Karin in preschool.

Mary Kristen had just celebrated her first birthday. Mary made a cake for her and I was the mean father and took her bottle away. She was handling liquids well from a cup and I saw no need to continue with the bottle.

With the children being so close in age, they got along quite well together. I had a Gracie who cared for the children while I was teaching. One night a week my oldest son needed an allergy injection and people from the church brought in supper. Now that I was dating, they prepared food for all nine of us.

Because Mary was in the process of a divorce, her attorney said that we needed to date very publicly. Thus we went to concerts together, out to dinner with other people and in February began attending church together with all nine of us. There were many expressions of support for us dating. Several people indicated to me that it was great that I was providing a mother for the children. I appreciated their response, but strongly felt God's hand in what was happening. I clearly did not go out looking for a mother for my children. I sought a relationship with someone who could become a teammate, that we could share our life together. Mary and I both knew the day would come when the children would move out and establish their own homes. Finding someone to care for the children would be looking for a "housekeeper". I already had Gracie capably fulfilling that role.

As we looked at blending families, it was time to decide where we should live. Neither house was suited for seven children. I was working in the school on the north side of Holland, a different district from Mary's children. Someone's children would have to move to a different school. The negotiation began. Because my house could be adjusted easiest we decided to build a bedroom in the basement for the three boys. Looking back we knew that it was very risky decision, because there was no egress window in the basement. We knew that this was a temporary situation until we could build a larger home.

We decided to get married on April 30, 1971, a Friday afternoon in the parsonage of Third Reformed Church. I taught school that day, and we gathered at the parsonage with our children and good friends Harley and Phyllis Brown as witnesses. We wished to have this meaningful for the children without the distractions of other witnesses. Looking back, Mary and I both realized that our parents would have liked to have been part of that event.

After the ceremony we scattered children to various grandparents for the weekend so that we could enjoy some time alone. This was an adventure for us. We forgot our map, I forgot my watch and we were headed toward unknown places. The first night we spent in a hotel in Benton Harbor, Michigan about an hour's drive from home. Saturday morning we had breakfast and then drove into downtown Chicago. We had reservations in Hammond, Indiana not realizing it was a long ways from Chicago. The logistics of this weekend did not provide us with relaxation but rather it was a weekend with a lot of driving, going nowhere. We decided that next time we would find a hotel in downtown Chicago to better enjoy the sights and sounds of the city.

At six o'clock on Sunday evening all the children gathered around the table for supper. The seven children all looked like they would be play actors in the musical Oliver, sitting around the table singing "food, glorious food". Blending two families meant differences in eating habits. We decided that everyone would benefit by structure, mealtimes would occur as close to 5:30 as possible and that rules of the house would be clearly stated. Following supper, I sat down with everyone and told them the following:

Breakfast would be served at 7:30 AM, everyone eating the same food.

In order to be ready for breakfast, all children needed to be dressed, and all beds made.

The older boys would take their regular bus to school, Mary would drive the two older girls into town, so they could go to the school they had been attending.

Because Mary was a student at Hope College, we would continue with Gracie being the housekeeper, caring for the three younger children.

When I got home from school I would start supper with the food that was assigned for the day. Each week the meals would be mapped out, assuring that the grocery shopping provided the ingredients for all meals.

Bed times would be determined by age appropriateness. Sunday night's all children were in bed by eight o'clock, because mom and dad were tired and we wanted everyone rested for the next week.

My home had a portable dishwasher adequate for holding and cleaning all the dishes for one meal. This meant a lot of creativity in loading the dishwasher to get the dishes clean. The laundry room had a washer and dryer and a separate tub called a "suds saver" cutting down on the amount of soap needed to do laundry. With the volume of laundry we soon discovered that the septic tank was overflowing every time we did laundry. Pumping out the tank only brought temporary relief. After two years of living in this house we decided it was necessary to look for something larger.

We took rides to look at neighborhoods. We consulted with realtors to determine the value of our home, and what the cost differential would be if we moved into something larger. Conversations with school officials helped us determine which elementary school would best meet our needs. Because we had two children in fourth grade, two children in second grade, a first grader, one child attending kindergarten along with a preschooler we wanted to make sure that there were enough classes for the older children to have their own teacher.

We made a decision to have a house built. We chose a plan from the Sunday papers that had five bedrooms with 2 1/2 baths. A living room, dining room, family room and kitchen on the first floor along with a laundry room would suit our needs. We found a builder who had 41 houses in the process of being built. He mostly used his own building plans, but was willing to use our design. He took out a sheet of notebook paper, wrote down the various allowances for appliances, carpeting, countertops, tile, driveway and doors and windows, giving a talley of $41,500 including the price of the property. We agreed to the price and with a handshake we had a "gentleman's agreement". He built our home according to the specifications allowing us to participate in painting and staining the interior walls. Apart from this we also did the landscaping which provided considerable "sweat equity".

Breaking ground in January we were able to move into the home in July. This home served us well for 34 years until our children encouraged us to go into a condo because they were concerned I would fall down the stairs. I was diagnosed with

Parkinson's disease five years ago; a move to a condo has been a good one.

As I look back on those early years, I remember that it took considerable energy to raise a large family. We were told that large families do not take vacations or eat out at restaurants. We did take vacations and we would go out to dinner especially to restaurants that had a buffet.

As we have discussed those early years with our children we have learned that with the authoritarian strategies that I imposed, compensation was made. When I said that all beds had to be made before breakfast, I learned that the older boys made the bed of their younger brother. When I said that all mealtimes were together, I learned later that in the middle of the night one of the boys would go down to the kitchen to eat cereal, because he was so hungry.

Over the years I transitioned from an authoritarian model of parenting to utilizing the Family Council. That material is covered in a separate chapter.

7

RUNNING AWAY FROM HOME FAMILY VACATIONS

Our first family vacation occurred the summer of 1971 after we were newly married. We introduced our family to camping. While a tent would have been a big stretch, we chose to rent a pop up camper to sleep all nine of us. Off we went in the wood grained panel station wagon to Glen Lake in northern Michigan looking just like Chevy Chase.

Because our youngest was a little more than a year old we had to take along a high chair and a porta -crib. We carried a minimum amount of clothes because there wasn't much room to pack. We had three girls sleeping on one end of the camper, two boys who slept on the table that pulled down, the youngest in the porta crib and one boy sleeping on a bench. Mary and I were in one of the foldout wings. When it was time for bed, we stored the highchair in the car. Thus, when we wanted to go for a ride, we had to take items out of the car and put them in the camper.

Each child was given a structured painted beer crate, decorated and personalized. In it they would put their clothes and anything else they want to take along on the trip

At night, before bedtime, a campfire provided a cozy time to enjoy smores.

 Mary and I would sit outside wrapped up in a blanket, waiting for the children to go to sleep. During the day all of us enjoyed the water and climbing the sand dunes. Because Mary enjoyed sewing, we made a trip to Traverse Bay Woolens. This vacation gave us good bonding time as well as a lot of fun. We also introduced fishing and canoeing to the children. In future years whenever we would ask where the children would like to go on vacation, the answer was always Glen Lake.

A TRIP TO CANADA

One summer we were given the offer to use a cottage in Canada about 100 miles north and east of Toronto. The cost was $100. a week. We packed up all seven children and the family dog Daisy. Again we were in the nine passenger station wagon. The cottage we went to was on 12 Mile Lake near the towns of Minden, Carnarvon and Haliburton. Our plan was to stay about 10 days.

The small black-and-white TV had one channel, the Canada Broadcasting network. This limited television watching. Video games had not been invented. We arrived on Saturday. The next day, we went to church with our family filling two of the ten pews. The United Church of Canada service was very interesting.

This cottage was on a beautiful lake with crystal-clear water. The lake overall was quite shallow, but deep enough for the children to dive off from the dock.

It's Time to Clean the Basement Again

On a rainy day, Mary went into town to inquire about an Indian reservation. We had been told that there was a large reservation nearby. We of course, had our preconceived notion of what it would look like. When we arrived we saw many men in black leather jackets riding motorcycles. There were no beads for sale and their general store was like any other.

During my training as a social worker, I heard that it takes seven days being away on vacation to begin feeling relaxed. Of a seven day vacation, the seventh day is actually the first day of vacation. It takes six days to burn stresses out of your system. While we had contracted for 10 days away, we called the cottage owner and asked to extend our stay by a week. When that was agreed upon, we went to the bank to borrow money on our credit card, to be able to buy more groceries and stay the extra time. Of course the premium for borrowing on the credit card was high, but we felt it worthwhile.

Our children played board games, and one night put on a skit for us somewhat like they had done in their Christian summer camp. Creativity ran rampant. All of us let our "little kid" out to play. As parents, we didn't realize we had so much talent in our children. Now we realized that it was a taste of what was to come. I remember being able to sit and read an entire book, cover to cover, in a relatively short amount of time.
All of us took turns doing dishes, taking the dog for a walk and in general, supporting one another, since we had no neighbors, no telephone and no interruptions. We had our own "On Golden Pond".

You really have to like each other as a family to be able to spend eighteen days in a remote area in Northern Canada. We think we succeeded nicely.

ATLANTIC CITY, NEW JERSEY 1972

Serving as president of the local Education Association, I was to go to the National Education Association annual conference in Atlantic City, New Jersey. The local organization would pay for my flight and lodging, but I chose to take our family along by renting a camper. Our youngest child did not go along, because she was very young. (We still hear from her that she didn't get to go on this trip).

My days were spent in meetings at the Atlantic City conference center. I would leave in the morning, spend the day in meetings and return to the campground at night. Because there was another teacher from Holland at the campground, we did some carpooling. This gave Mary the use of a car some of the days. And it rained, and rained. Did I say it rained? How much can you entertain children in a pop-up tent camper? My days were spent in interesting meetings and Mary entertained children. She played games, board games and creative crafts for four days while it rained all day. After the fourth day she said she couldn't do it one more day with rain. I was able to carpool, and then she eagerly used the car

DENVER, COLORADO LATE 1970'S

As a school social worker, I was encouraged to attend a conference in Denver Colorado. We knew that camping was not an option. Again I took the money that would be used for flight and hotel and brought the family along. Friends of ours found a reasonable hotel. (I think it was not a very reputable hotel, because people seemed to be coming and going quite frequently)

In preparation for the trip we were told that there were few radio stations in Iowa and Nebraska. We had purchased a 12 passenger van that had an AM radio. We replaced that with an AM/FM/ tape player radio, with speakers mounted in the front and the back. We recorded some of our LP records on cassette tape. We would then have music where there were no radio stations. We listen to ABBA and John Denver *"Rocky Mountain High"*.

On the way to Colorado we stayed in Sioux City, Iowa with my brother and his family. Traveling across Iowa is not the most interesting; traveling across Nebraska was about the same.

We arrived at our Denver hotel in the dark. Getting up the next morning, we saw the glorious mountains.

Because this was spring break, the children did not miss any school.

Never having been to Colorado, we said that we wanted to go up the mountain to see the ski resorts. It was April and the resorts were open. What we did not figure on, was the road not being open. We waited during the day for Loveland Pass to open, after a heavy snowfall. We all piled in the van, turned on John Denver and headed up the mountain. Having had no experience driving in the mountains, I was rather tense. As we were climbing, we saw a bus ahead of us. We realized that we had to go in the same direction. We kept climbing, climbing and more climbing until we reached a high point, then stopped to see the skiers. On the return trip the van was an eerily quiet, as all of us were rather uneasy on roads with no guard rails. On several occasions, I pulled off to take pictures of the beautiful scenery. (When we had the pictures developed, none of them turned out, because the camera was broken).

One of the dinners out we had was at a Mexican restaurant where a diver would climb up to a platform about 12 feet up and dive into a tank below. This reminded us of the cliff divers we had heard about, off the coast of Mexico.

Among the highlights in Denver was visiting the mint where money was made. Mary took the kids there while I was in meetings.

I have found it very rewarding to be able to share in travel with our family. On several occasions, I could have traveled alone and had a very relaxing and enriching experience. Being able to share with Mary and the children, was a bonus, because most of the cost of the trips was equal to what it would've cost for me to go alone. And we now had shared memories.

RETRACING A TRIP OUT EAST

When I was a student at Hope College, in my junior year as a member of the Chapel Choir, we traveled during spring vacation out East beginning in London, Ontario then traveling to Rochester, New York and Albany, New York, traveling down the Hudson River stopping along the way to visit Hyde Park. Eventually we were in New York City then on to New Jersey, Pennsylvania and then back to Holland.

Typical for these trips, we stayed in the homes of church members where we would offer a concert. In the evening, dinner was often served in the church. We would sing the concert and then be taken by our hosts to their home. We then would be expected to converse with them about Hope College. With much travel on a bus, sightseeing, singing concerts and sleeping in different beds every night, we were tired after the evening concert.

I stayed at a home in Hamilton, Ontario where the family spoke little English. The man of the house would say "Mama, coffee" or "Mama, slippers". His wife would get the coffee or slippers. This was a significant cultural difference for me. I can never imagine my father demanding "coffee or slippers" of my mother.

Whenever possible we were allowed to stay with someone we knew. My sister-in-law's parents, grandparents, uncle and aunt all lived on the same farm in Berne, New York. Several of my classmates and I stayed with them because they had many empty bedrooms.

In New York City we stayed in a hotel and I remember spending a significant amount of money to go see the play "My Fair Lady".

One year I suggested that as a family we follow somewhat the same path our Chapel Choir had traveled and, wherever possible stay with families. This was one trip we took during spring break. We drove through Canada and stayed the first night in Buffalo, New York. I showed the children where we had sung in the church in Rochester, New York. We then went across on the New York State Thruway to Berne, New York where we stayed with the same family I had stayed with when I was in college. They were wonderful hosts taking us out to a restaurant for dinner in the evening and then scattering us to three different houses to sleep. Grandpa and grandma were about 100 years old at this time, yet still vibrant and able to comfortably house some of the children. Their son-in-law, a man who actively worked the farm showed the children how to tap maple trees for syrup, and then he showed how it is boiled down to be ready for the table. That morning we were offered pancakes, cold or hot cereal, eggs and bacon, fresh fruit or juice and whatever else we wanted, and plenty of it. No one walked away from breakfast hungry!

We then were taken on a tour of a woman's home where the lady made Easter eggs. We were told this was one of the largest collections in the United States. Near our hosts home there were Caverns. We were introduced to the formations found underground. I still don't know the difference between stalactites and stalagmites. The family paid our admission to the Caverns and then brought us to the local historical buildings. We were given a tour of the historical museum where the family had invested many volunteer hours.

We stayed at second night with this family because they were so very gracious and we really enjoyed their company. They were in a remote area and didn't get many visitors other than family.

The next day we traveled down the Hudson River stopping at Hyde Park reflecting the experience I had when I was in college. I wished to have the children see a piece of history as well as the affluence that many families experienced on the East Coast.

Our next stop was to spend an evening in Connecticut with Matthew and Carol Lynn, a couple we knew previously living in Holland. They prepared a dinner of spaghetti and meatballs with garlic toast and salad. All of us participated in cleanup. They were very gracious in providing housing for all nine of us.

Our next stop on the agenda was to go to New York City. Matthew indicated it would be difficult getting into New York because of a transit strike. There were no taxis, buses or subways running. We had come this far and didn't want to be disappointed. Against his advice to stay out of the city, we left Connecticut with some anxiety that this leg of the trip would not be accomplished. We discovered that this first day of the transit strike was also the first day of Passover. Thus all Jewish people stayed home. Many other people also stayed home. We were able to breeze through the city seeing many sites. We saw:

- the Statue of Liberty
- the Cathedral of St. John the Divine
- Grand Central Station
- Little Italy
- Chinatown
- Fifth Avenue including Sak's, Macy's and all of the electronics stores.
- We stopped for lunch many of us having a fresh bagel and cream cheese.
- We found Madison Square Garden

- We saw the Empire State Building
- All of this was accomplished in one day.

I could hear myself saying like Chevy Chase "hey kids, there's..."

Our final stop was in New Jersey, where we stayed with Mary's friends from the University of Michigan now working near New York City.

This trip was a growing experience for our family. We learned how other people live and work. The 100 year old couple lived to each celebrate their 105th birthdays and on their 78 wedding anniversary their maid of honor had lunch with them. Our costs were less because we stayed in people's homes. That was quite an experience with seven children. Not many people can accommodate nine extra bodies in their homes.

Planning for this trip was essential, for we needed to have enough money for gas, food and the unexpected surprises that might occur. I especially appreciated being able to share my college experience of being out east and connecting with people from various walks of life. Traveling to Hyde Park was telling the children about a piece of history and one of our presidents. We saw the Stock Market since Mary's father was a stock broker. There were several things we didn't do such as go to the top of the Empire State Building – dad was afraid of heights, so was mom.

It's Time to Clean the Basement Again

Again "a joy or a sorrow is not complete until it is shared". We together shared in a joy of mine and we are all richer for it.

8

LEGACY

Through the years, one of the issues that we have been most forthright about is legacy. Providing ways to continue what we, as parents, have established in our family was a goal. This comes out of a history of hearing stories about our ancestors and hoping to be able to continue those stories with our children.

Several years ago, I gathered the family history. The paternal DeWitt family history was gained by sitting down with Aunt Emma and a tape recorder and just having a conversation that lasted about an hour to an hour and a half. During that time, we talked freely about the early history of the DeWitt family. Her father, my Grandpa DeWitt died of pneumonia when my dad was two years old leaving a widow with three children. Much of the family connection was lost because my grandmother's family pretty much adopted my father. This aunt and uncle cared for him until high school. I remember my grandmother as a very stoic person, but after hearing the family story, I gained a new insight.

My grandpa ran a hardware store in Muskegon Heights called The Buckley Hardware. When he died, there were many people who owed the family money. So, Grandma DeWitt went into the bars on Friday afternoons to get money from the paychecks of the men who owed my grandpa, before they spent it on liquor. She was looking out for her family and knew what would happen if these men spent the evening at the bar. My father was raised by an aunt and uncle in Spring Lake and then returned home, to attend Junior High and High School and was graduated from Muskegon Heights High School.

When my wife Jan died, my mother used an expression, "Oh, those poor orphaned children." My father turned beet red and now I understand why. Because he was orphaned himself, he didn't want my children to have that kind of negative image. He was looking for any way possible for the children to be maintained as a family unit and not have to see one of them go and live with a relative. That was not an option that I considered, but it was a strong concern that he had because of his own family history. A family history explains how people behave and how children respond.

On my maternal grandparent's side, I remember my grandmother always insisting that if we came in through the front door, we leave by the front door. She felt that if you come in through one door and leave through another, you bring company. Whether that was an Old Norwegian folk tale or just an idiosyncrasy that she had I don't know. I find myself constantly following the model. Eric Burne, in his book, *What Do You Say After You Say, Hello?* suggests that we learn many messages from our grandparents, and from their history.

I remember my Grandmother Anderson always saying, "Don't say 'can't' before you try."

If my wife asks me to fix the bicycle, I try, because of grandma's saying. My wife had asked me to fix the washing machine. I tried and didn't do very well. Finally, I gave up and called a repairman. These messages we receive from our grandparents can become overwhelming and handicapping, but recognizing the message as an imprint is important for all of us. After some time in our development, we realize that we cannot be a person for all seasons and need to make decisions on what we can and cannot do.

But early on, I was trying to do everything because grandmother said "Don't say 'can't' before you try."

In 1989 I asked my Aunt Ruth to write the Anderson family history. As she wrote the history by hand, I typed her writings. With my mother coming from a family of seven children, there were many aunts and uncles whose stories I did not know. Aunt Ruth provided that information. Over all, the family history was a clean history. One uncle had been married several times and she had him only married once. (In the appendix you will find the Anderson family history).

I remember my aunt telling me that my grandparents homesteaded 80 acres and that they started in the middle of their property, slashing and burning and clearing to be able to make farmland. Starting in the middle meant that in time all the land was exposed and the neighbors were astounded by the size of the property. In time, Grandpa Anderson divided the land with his children, giving one daughter who did not marry a larger portion. She continued to care for her mother and father in their old age. Each child could decide what to do with his/her property. All of them eventually sold their property and it has become a development of 10-acre plots. There seemed to be a sense of equity that everyone was taken care of fairly.

My Aunt Ruth was a spiritual grandparent to me. She would always tell me that she was praying for me and that she included in her prayers the names of all our children and grandchildren. This piece of legacy was important to me.

 One Sunday she often invited us for dinner. She hosted a dinner with very fine Franciscan ware Desert Rose dishes. Preparing all the food for the nine of us, having two meats, two vegetables, two kinds of potatoes and two kinds of desserts was a common occurrence. There were many choices.

Mary asked Aunt Ruth if she had a deck of cards for the children to play with one afternoon and she said there were no cards in the house. They were called 'devil cards'. That led us into a conversation so we could understand why.

My grandparents were raised Lutheran in Norway and remained Lutheran after they immigrated here. My grandpa drank, smoked and gambled and spent money in ways that were not appropriate for the head of a family. Then my grandparents went to a camp meeting where they heard a message that compelled them to give up their bad habits. My grandfather gave up smoking, drinking and gambling and from that day on, never once smoked again. My grandmother gave her wedding ring and her girdle to missions because it says in scripture that you are not to "adorn yourself with gold or to be bound up". I'm not sure that is a good literal translation of that passage but it had an impact on my grandmother.

The children found Grandfather's clay pipe out in the field one day and he just turned aside and said, "That has no meaning for me, please throw it away." Thus there were no cards or smoking in the house.

That piece of family history/legacy has been part of my core as I have made decisions. That does not mean that decisions are always in accordance with what my grandparents did, but there is always a small voice telling me that this is a model. With our own children, we did several things over the years to maintain a sense of legacy. Every Christmas, I wrote the children a Christmas letter that partially outlined my journey during the past year, and where I had seen them growing and developing and just some hints or nudges for them in their lives. With that, I often included a book. Of course, every year the children would moan and groan, saying, "What is Dad reading this year?"

Some of the books I find still on their shelves. Some they have read; others I'm not sure about. But probably one of the most important books I gave to them was a book by Gary Smalley, *The Blessing,* now a new edition *The Gift of the Blessing.* In their annual letter, I wanted to affirm to the children that I loved them and that we were doing our best as parents to give them the blessing and that they, through this nurturing, would be free to celebrate with joy the faith they have. Another book was by Jerry Jampolsky *Love is Letting Go of Fear.* I picked that book up in California, read it in three hours on the airplane on the way to Chicago, and knew it was not a difficult read. I continue to suggest this book as I work with people because it helps to relieve themselves of guilt and conflict when there is forgiveness work that has to be done. There were additional books that were given through the years, such as *Jacob the Baker*.

Family pictures capture the clothing styles and haircuts of the time.

Being a blended family, we looked for opportunities to celebrate together. As the children grew we celebrated birthdays, anniversaries, etc. On our 25th wedding anniversary, we had everyone home and invited our family and friends to celebrate with us in a special recommitment service at church with a reception afterward. Because our wedding was very small and intimate, with only the children and a close couple as attendants, we felt that we would like to share the joy that we had in a recommitment ceremony with a larger group of people. We had a special dinner at a fine restaurant and gave each of the children a gift. The girls received identical necklaces. The boys received a clock with the date engraved... These objects did not cost us a lot of money but they were a piece of what we would call "building legacy".

Sometime later, we set a goal and then wrote a letter to our children and grandchildren inviting them to go on a trip with us for our 30th wedding anniversary. Both Mary and I were turning 60 in 2001 and we asked them to set aside time for a week-long vacation that we could enjoy together. We would pay their flight, hotel, ground transportation and entrances to theme parks. Thus 27 of our family all flew into Orange County, John Wayne airport in California on Saturday, June 23, 2001 and gathered at a hotel with a nice swimming pool. We spent time around the pool eating pizza and talking about our week. On Sunday morning we attended worship together at the Crystal Cathedral where I had heard my call to ministry through a men's conference in February 1992. We called ahead to the Crystal Cathedral and were given reserved seats and several of us had the opportunity to greet Dr. Schuler between services. He was more than gracious in affirming our lives as a family. From there we went to Disneyland and spent Sunday afternoon there. On Monday we were at California Adventure. Staying right across from the Disneyland Park, we were able to come and go as we wanted. One of Mary's goals was to have all the children go on the *"It's a Small World"* ride. All the children gathered after the Disney parade and we were together in two boats going through that display. Many years ago we had gone to Florida as a family in the wood grained panel station wagon carrying our own food in because we could not afford the lunch inside the theme park. We of course went on the ride *"It's a Small World"* in Florida.

One of our children said, "Now, Mom, you'll have no regrets because you got your wish to go on the '*It's a Small World'*."

Even though there is some corniness to that expression, it is very meaningful to find you can have all of your family together for an event, especially, such a large family. On Tuesday morning, we went to Rodeo Drive for the children to experience the sight of three Rolls Royce cars in a row. There was significant affluence. We saw where movies are filmed and where the rich and famous live. It was quite exciting. From there, we went down the coast to Ensenada, Mexico. We stayed in Mexico overnight and then drove an hour and a half up the mountain to the orphanage Rancho Santa Marta, where Mary and I had done a mission work project. We arrived there and visited the orphanage cottages where some of the children live. We met some of the house parents and saw the meal preparation. We looked at the layout of this mission that Bill and Kay Lawrence serve. Our children took up a collection of the money they would have given us for the year as gifts and gave it as a gift to the orphanage. This probably bought two or three months worth of groceries.

We returned to Ensenada and had a lovely family dinner together and then went on to San Diego for the remainder of the week. We visited the Zoo, Wild Animal Park and Lego Land. All of these events we were able to pay for by making the decision to shift priorities. That year, the children did not receive Christmas, birthday or anniversary gifts. All of us had a wonderful experience. How freeing it was not to have to be thinking about what small gift we would buy for a child for Christmas, especially when we see that our children have most of the things they need. What a meaningful time it was for all of us to be together and celebrate family closeness with everyone paying family rent and having fun as a family. Our real goal was to be able to give it away.

I've seen a bumper sticker that says, "We are spending our children's inheritance". I take issue with that expression, because I feel we were celebrating and putting something in the bank that far exceeds any monetary gift. This was a way we were able to continue to build legacy for them. It is my belief that this gift of time and energy and connectedness will pay far more benefits than if we had exchanged gifts for the year, because this became a storehouse of memories.

We are especially grateful that we were able to enjoy this trip before the tragedy of September 11, 2001, because I'm not sure anyone would be very comfortable flying with the whole family on the plane together. We did not feel fear as we departed from the airport, but felt a real sense of gratitude for the way God had guided us through our lives together.

Someone said that 80% of the goals that you write down, you accomplish. This was one goal that we wrote down. I found the letter written to the children outlining what we would do and it was interesting to see how many of the events that we did, fell in line with what I had written in that letter. The children's contribution on the trip was to pay for their own meals. Most often we pooled our resources to order takeout pizza, sub-sandwiches, etc. You can imagine what the bill for eight hotel rooms looked like. The cost of getting into Disneyland was $1,700 for 26 bodies. Yet, that investment, again, is one that is hoped will pay off in dividends for years.

Each year, we attempt to plan at least a week when most of the family is available. When families become scattered throughout the country, it is difficult to have any kind of vacation time together. During our children's teenage years, there were times when we would go with whoever was available. Now, we do our best to aim for a week in the summer when the majority of us can be together. It was our hope that for our 35th wedding anniversary, in another four years, we would be able to do some kind of family gathering. This could possibly be at a theme park or large resort where everyone could come and go and enjoy their time together, but also where we could have time for relationship building and time to be able to reconnect with each other.(Note: We did go back to California for the 35th Anniversary)

After a recent week of being together, I was driving down the road thinking that I am the richest man in the world. I am very fortunate to have healthy children and grandchildren who all seem to like each other and enjoy spending time with each other and who all are connected in some way within a faith community. Each family unit attends worship on a regular basis, probably at least three out of four Sundays a month. They are involved in small groups and other service activities and find ways to give back to the community what they have been given. It is exciting to see your children elected to an office, bringing their children to church for a baptism, or reaching out to a family in need. What a blessing to know that they are sharing what they are gaining in their experiences within their faith community.

If a parent shares his or her spiritual journey, sometimes that can cause a child to feel inadequate. Yet it does set a model that it is accepted behavior to share your spiritual journey. Therefore, our children do share with us where they are growing spiritually.

A PIECE OF LEGACY FROM A GRANDPARENT
In the summer of 1985, my mother was dying of leukemia. In previous years she had disposed of all of her worldly possessions which were of value. The following letter was written to her grandchildren.

It's Time to Clean the Basement Again
Dear grandchildren of Martha DeWitt,

During the last three weeks that Grandma knew she was failing, she talked about her various properties and how they should be divided. We made a list and honored all of her wishes.

When talking about her car, she said "All the grandchildren would love it".

In 1978, Grandma DeWitt bought a 1974 Dodge Dart SE with 42,000 miles on it, for $2200 cash. I sold the car with 53,800 miles for $1450. Thus the difference was $750 for seven years use. During the seven years, there were very few repairs necessary, and the car was kept in mint condition.

I have noticed in Grandma's checkbook that the first check she wrote every month after payday was her check to the church. In many ways she was a good steward of her resources, not complaining, but satisfied with what she had.

The enclosed check is $1430 divided 11 ways less $20 used for selling the car. Please use this money for something special that will have lasting value and memories for you. It was decided this money could be well used by all grandchildren.

Love Uncle Denny -- Dad

AN ADDENDUM TO LEGACY

Friends of ours from Pensacola, Florida, invited me to perform a wedding ceremony for their daughter Beth Anne in July 2007. On the Sunday afternoon, preceding the Friday wedding, Lynn and Wayne brought two vessels of water to be blessed. They had collected water from Loch Ness, Scotland

and Loch Neigh, Northern Ireland, where their daughter and future son-in-law met. This water was then blessed and given to the children at the wedding reception, to be used for the baptism of their children and to be shared with good friends.

Wayne had traveled to Scotland previously to research the family tree, and found the clan identification clothing and some of their history. The water that was given to the young couple provides another link in the family story.

Water is used for cleansing, and water is a significant Biblical symbol. The Bible speaks of flowing streams, parting the seas, walking on water, foot washing, and of course the waters used for baptism. The following liturgy was used for the blessing of the waters.

Blessing of the Waters from the Hamilton Clan
July 15, 2007
Hebrews 2:11-2:18

[11]For the one who sanctifies and those who are sanctified all have one Father.* For this reason Jesus* is not ashamed to call them brothers and sisters,* [12]saying, 'I will proclaim your name to my brothers and sisters,* in the midst of the congregation I will praise you.'

[13]And again 'I will put my trust in him.'And again, 'Here am I and the children whom God has given me.'

14 Since, therefore, the children share flesh and blood, he himself likewise shared the same things, so that through death he might destroy the one who has the power of death, that is, the devil, [15]and free those who all their lives were held in slavery by the fear of death. [16]- For it is clear that he did not come to help angels, but the descendants of Abraham. [17]Therefore he had to become like his brothers and sisters* in every respect, so that he might be a merciful and faithful high priest in the service of God, to make a sacrifice of atonement for the sins of the people. [18]Because he himself was tested by what he suffered, he is able to help those who are being tested.

It's Time to Clean the Basement Again

That these waters may be sanctified by the power, and effectual operation, and descent of the Holy Spirit,

Let us pray to the Lord.

That there may descend upon these waters the cleansing operation of the super-substantial Trinity,

Let us pray to the Lord.

That this water may be unto the healing of souls and bodies, and unto the banishing of every hostile power

Let us pray to the Lord.

That the Lord our God will send down the blessing of Jordan, and sanctify these waters,

Let us pray to the Lord.

For all those who entreat God for protection,

Let us pray to the Lord.

That he will illumine us with the light of understanding, with the consubstantial Trinity,

Let us pray to the Lord.

That the Lord our God will show us forth sons and heirs of his kingdom, through partaking of and sprinkling with these waters,

Let us pray to the Lord.

We especially pray for John and Beth Anne, that the legacy of this family will follow them, through these waters as they establish their own family.

Our Father who art in Heaven, Hallowed be thy name, Thy Kingdom come, Thy will be done on earth as it is in Heaven.

Give us this day our daily bread,

And forgive us our sins as we forgive those who sin against us.

And lead us not into temptation, but deliver us from evil.

For thine is the kingdom and the power and the glory forever. AMEN

From the Episcopal Book of Common Prayer, edited

72

9

BE THOU MY VISION

It is my belief that music is one form of expression of the Holy Spirit. Two significant hymns have recurred in my life.

In August of 1970, my wife Jan died of cancer. At her funeral we sang two hymns: "Our God, Our Help in Ages Past" and "Be Thou My Vision." As time went on these hymns kept appearing in my life and nudging me when I was looking for direction.

A year later as I worshiped at Fourth Presbyterian Church in Chicago, with my wife Mary, the trumpets blasted with the "trompette au shamaude," the first verse of "Our God Our Help in Ages Past."

A short time later on the Sunday that Mary graduated from Hope College, the hymn in church was "Be Thou My Vision." On several occasions after this hymn was sung in church on Sunday and an event of major significance happened during the week.

On the Sunday before my father died we sang "Be Thou My Vision."

On the Sunday when our son Mark graduated from college we sang "Be Thou My Vision."

On the Sunday before my mother died we sang "Be Thou My Vision." This hymn reoccurred often enough that we knew that there was some deeper meaning. Both of our sons used it at their weddings. A niece used it at the end of her wedding. She had been very close to Jan and wanted to honor her in this way.

On a Sunday in January of 1992 we sang "Be Thou My Vision." On the Thursday following, my sister-in-law called to say that her granddaughter Lisa had died from SIDS.

That following Sunday, we attended a memorial service for Lisa and sang "Children of the Heavenly Father "and "Jesus Loves Me."

On the next Sunday at Third Reformed Church we sang the opening hymn as recorded in the bulletin. Scripture was read and Dr. Dennis Voskuil announced that the middle hymn would be changed to "Jesus Loves Me" rather than the printed number. Third Reformed Church always does things "decently and in order" and this certainly was a diversion from their usual practice. I was in the choir loft and Mary was down front. We could hardly sing, our grief was so great. After church we both agreed that this was a strong nudge from the Holy Spirit. I will explain it in more detail to follow.

On Wednesday morning after that Sunday, I got on the plane to travel to a Men's Conference at the Crystal Cathedral. On Thursday we sat at tables of eight. I opened the song sheet and number four was "Be Thou My Vision." I mentioned the story to the man sitting at my right and indicated I might need some help when we would sing that song. Thursday all went well, Friday also, and then came Saturday night. We had dinner and then came the closing activities. Ken Medema, a blind pianist/composer began the evening with "Be Thou My Vision." After a short time there was a slideshow of the conference participants in casual conversation and in meetings. On the screen was a slide of a pastor from Chino, California, and me. Ken Medema was playing "Be Thou My Vision" and then modulated into "Jesus Loves Me." The man sitting next to me said I better have my ear to the ground because something was happening.

I called my wife Mary that night and told her of the events of that evening and indicated I would likely be quitting my job to go into the ministry. This was no surprise her and she has been very supportive on my journey. On the day I was ordained you can imagine what we sang.

This hymn and others change meaning each time they are sung, because our spiritual journey is continually evolving. Unless we are willing to grow spiritually, we are frozen in our ability to sense the working of the Holy Spirit.

Can it be explained logically?
No.
 Can it be explained spiritually?
 Yes
Being a spiritual person means that your eyes and ears are open to signs and the singing around you. Your heart and mind need to be open to God.

In February of 2010 I was in church standing next to Avis when we sang "Be thou My Vision" and the pianist modulated into "Jesus Loves Me". On the first Sunday in March the prelude and postlude were different settings of "Be Thou My Vision" and the offertory was "Jesus Loves Me". Where is God calling me now? This book is a form of expression that explains my journey of growth and meaning.

10

WHY DO I ALWAYS HAVE TO GO TO BED AT 7:30?"

This comment came from our youngest daughter, Mary Kristen who was probably three or four years old and was upset because she saw her older brothers and sisters going to bed later than she was. This daughter had some health problems and needed a little extra sleep. When someone in our family said, "How about 7:31?" she got very excited and said, "Oh, hurray, that sounds really great!"

To a child this age, this seemed like a giant change and she was very appreciative. We still joke about Mary Kristen going to bed at 7:31 and being excited about it.

This all came about in a family meeting. These family meetings were convened once a week, often on Thursday night from 6:30 until 7:30. The time limit for our family meeting was always one hour.

This concept began several years ago when I was attending a graduate class in social work in a Grand Rapids, Michigan, satellite campus of the University of Michigan. In this class there was a woman from Muskegon Heights whose husband was a banker. This woman and her husband, and their two children, had weekly family meetings to discuss their schedule, the needs of the children, and to plan for future events. I got very excited about this idea one night and came home to suggest it to my wife. Her response was, "We are going to do what?" I responded, "Well, the concept of family council sounds good to me." We discussed this for three or four months, did some research, and decided to launch our own family council meeting.

Initially, there were many fears. Typically, on a Sunday, I would say to the kids, "Hey kids, let's go to the John Ball Park Zoo." We would get in the car, go see the animals and there would be grumbling and complaining on the way there and back home. "Why do I always have to sit in the way-back?" "I'm thirsty," "I'm tired," "I'm sweaty," or "Why do we have to go smell those stinky animals?" This would be a family outing that would end in disaster.

Once we started scheduling family council meetings, everyone in the family received one vote. For any motion to pass there had to be consensus or total agreement. In a large family of nine people, eight people could not gang up on one. Eight people could not say, "Dad has to take out the garbage" because Dad got one veto vote as did everyone else. Sometimes this would lead to lengthy meetings, but the concept allowed for much dialogue and negotiation.

As we launched these family council meetings, we set some rules.

First of all, everyone would sit on the floor, even Mom and Dad. That is an equalizer. It also meant that the duration of the meeting couldn't go terribly long because Mom and Dad couldn't sit on the floor for much more than an hour.

We changed the chairperson every session allowing everyone the leadership opportunity.

It's Time to Clean the Basement Again

Someone took minutes of the meeting and we had a some-what loose agenda that covered regular topics. First, we would have a jar where kids could put in their complaints. We would empty that jar of complaints. Second, we would talk about the schedule. We'd take out the weekly calendar and talk about who was going to the dentist, who needed to have a doctor's appointment, who needed new shoes, when a payday was coming, etc. There were various issues about scheduling vehicles and bodies.

We then planned for fun. Planning for fun is an important concept in family council because everyone can participate and feel that he or she is gaining something.

We would close with any additional issues that needed to be discussed. We would schedule our next meeting, but usually the meetings were pretty regular so everyone could count on that time.

Family Council is an Adlarian concept that comes out of a book that is entitled <u>Family Council.</u>

The book on family council is entitled "Family Council, the Dreikurs' Technique for Putting an End to War between Parents and Children, and Between Children and Children." It was formulated by Dr. Rudolph Dreikurs and carried on by his wife and children. This book was published after Rudolph Dreikurs died. He lived from 1897 to 1972.

As Mary and I read through the material, we found it to be a valuable resource. When we emptied the complaint jar, we would discuss, as a family, alternatives. Many things were discussed to the point of closure. Certainly, we all knew that an awareness of a problem was the first step toward bringing a solution. Second, we took a look at the schedule. Our dog was Daisy Dog. Daisy was a Christmas gift to our son Jim. Even though she was Jim's dog, everyone took turns walking the dog and taking care of her needs. We would schedule our "Dog Days." Whoever chose Monday would then walk the dog in the morning, afternoon and evening. He or she would make sure the dog was fed and could have the dog sleep with him or her that evening. A sign was put outside his or her bed- room door that read, "Daisy sleeps here." Additionally, this person took out the garbage, helped Mom in the kitchen, set the table and did whatever chores had to be done that day. With seven kids in the family and seven days in the week, "Daisy Dog Days" created a somewhat even dis- tribution of the work. Some days were more difficult than others, especially with invited guests. Therefore we changed "Daisy Dog Days" to equalize the workload.

The youngest age is the cheapest lesson

Being a blended family, we found it important that one child at a time be given special time with Mom, in the kitchen, in- teracting, helping with the tasks and generally assisting. A sibling could come to the kitchen and the special child would say, "You can't come into the kitchen, it's my special child day. I get time with Mom." Part of our motivation for this was that we said early on in our marriage that Mom or Dad should not be the *house slave*. There tends to be a lot of work that mothers and father do that require adult attention. Yet, it is extremely important to have children learn the tasks at a young age. It has been said **that the youngest age is the cheapest lesson.** Thus, children learning to work in the kit- chen, and learning that the forks go on the left and the knife and spoon on the right, are part of that early training that helped them realize how some systems work. Relating with Mom one to one was valuable bonding time.

One of my fondest recollections of a family meeting was the time when I announced that we had $150 to spend on a family outing and that we could go anywhere they wanted to go within our time frame. Mary and I suggested Thanksgiving weekend because we worked in public education and we had Friday, Saturday and Sunday available for the family. Immediately, the kids took out the atlas and figured out that we could go to Disney World in Florida and the $150 would get us there and back. As they began to do some investigating, they realized that both the amount of money and the time was inadequate for that kind of trip, Much energy went into horse-trading and figuring, budgeting, learning limits, boundaries, etc. The result of that particular planning session was that the whole family got into the wood-grained panel station wagon, went to Chicago on the day after Thanksgiving, saw the windows at Marshal Fields decorated for Christmas, ate out and did a little shopping. The $150 was used for gasoline, tolls, and food. We packed lunch and snacks. Everyone was allowed some spending money and the most beautiful part of that one-day trip to Chicago was the following benefit... **no one complained!** If I had announced that we were going to Chicago to see the windows at Marshal Fields, have dinner out, pack sandwiches and go for a three hour ride from home each way, there could have been considerable grumbling. Yet, because this was a decision made by everyone involved, no one grumbled. Everyone seemed to have a good time, and, to me, it was a very meaningful day. Logically, if you choose to go to downtown Chicago on a day when everyone is going to be there, it would be an insane decision. There was a lot of traffic and a lot of stop and go on the way. There were huge crowds, but everyone seemed to have a very good time. I still remember that as one of the symbols of what we were able to accomplish through family council.

We also had a wish list where everyone could say what he or she needed. Those who needed tennis shoes, boots, etc. would be put into the mixture of long range planning. This taught all of us to do some thinking ahead to what may be coming next. Young children don't typically do a lot of planning. These meetings helped all of us to think through our needs.

When we had family council meeting there was often grumbling. "Why do we have to have family council?" "Do we always have to have these meetings?" Some kids rebelled when they hit the teenage years. When one of our daughters went away to college, she said she was so pleased to leave home because she didn't have to do family council meetings any more. When she arrived at her college dorm, there appeared to be some chaos and within a couple of days, she rounded all of the suitemates together, sat down and had a family council meeting to decide who was going to clean the bathroom, take a shower in the morning or at night, etc., so that there was some organization to their lives. The one child who seemed to verbalize the most disgust with family council utilized the concept in her later life.

Some of our neighbors would observe what we were doing and one friend, especially, would often ask about family council. One day as we were going up north fishing I commented to Bob that I really enjoyed family council and he said to me, "If I hear from you one more time about family council, I'm probably not going to be your friend." Two weeks later, he came to me and said, "Dennis, I take those words back. Let's talk about family council."

Bob had two daughters. His wife and he were feeling overwhelmed with all the work that had to be done and they instituted a family council meeting. I still remember the result of one of their meetings where they listed all of the jobs that had to be done in the family and they each chose the jobs that they would do. Back that many years ago, there were some typical jobs assigned to men or women. At that time, men often washed the cars and women cleaned the stove. There was flip-flop in that family where Bob cleaned the stove, especially the oven, and his wife took care of the car. After cleaning the oven, Bob voted to immediately replace their stove with a self-cleaning oven. His wife had asked a number of times for a self-cleaning oven and he never saw the benefit of that. When he had to clean it, he realized how much difference that would make in their home.

Family council meetings help divide up the tasks that have to be done so no one person becomes the house slave. If many institutions were to use this kind of system, there would be a real benefit. Certainly, there could be long meetings for the negotiating that has to go on. Yet, when a limit is set on a meeting, it is amazing how much work is accomplished within that time. We rarely went beyond one hour for a family council meeting. We were able to accomplish a good amount of business in that amount of time by keeping notes and structuring the meeting the way we did. Everyone had a chance to participate as the chairman. Everyone had a chance to have his/her say. No one felt overpowered by someone else because there was an equalizer with no motions being passed without total agreement.

One of our regular features of meetings was the use of "budget sheets". Each child was to account for money spent in three categories: savings, spending and charity. The formula was save 10% give away 10% and the rest was available to spend. Weekly allowances were given when the budget sheet was presented to Dad. This was our attempt to bring balance to money management.

Some years later when the family had pretty much grown up and we no longer needed the family council meetings, we would occasionally sit down and talk about our schedule or some other issues. However, when the children were between the ages of five and sixteen, we conducted these meetings religiously. After the children were launched, Mary and I would sit down on Thursday nights and discuss the budget and what had to be done. That was still an important part of our week. Once we were at a point where we had more financial flexibility, we then did our cleaning on Thursday night. It's amazing how 6:00 on Thursday rolls around and it felt like there needed to be some productive work done during that time. So, as we did the cleaning on Thursday night, by Friday afternoon, we could kick back, relax and have a weekend unencumbered. Advanced planning, logically sitting down and thinking about what you have to do and organizing it, became for us a freeing experience.

11

NATURE VS NURTURE

Raising a blended family we were able to observe that you cannot deny nature, you cannot deny nurture. Each of us has our unique personality and certain behaviors that are inherent in our makeup. At one time I was the barber for the entire family and so there was a tendency for everyone to look somewhat alike, yet there were individual differences in hair color and somewhat different styles. This was done primarily for financial reasons.

Four of our children's mother died when they were ages seven years, five years, three years and eight months. The five and seven year old boys could remember certain behaviors of their mother. The two younger girls could not. When looking back at the three-year-old becoming a teenager, many traits of her mother emerged. When she was in 11th grade I would guess that her schedule of classes closely matched those her mother would've taken in the same grade. One similarity is both of them were in choir. Coursework would have been primarily a secretarial theme, typing, bookkeeping math and English. To my knowledge this was a case of more natural selection then it was guided with my input.

When I was in high school I played cello in the orchestra. One of my biological sons also played cello. Was that copycat behavior or was there something that naturally attracted him to cello? I did not play any sports, nor would I have been a good at sports, yet this son played football beginning with rocket football, continuing through high school and college, and postgraduate coaching football. His son excels in football, swimming and baseball.

On my maternal side of the family, many had musical talent. I sang in church choir while in high school and I continued to sing in a select choir in college. One granddaughter has inherited an outstanding voice and will likely use her gift professionally. Is that nature or is it nurture? Is that a result of training? Again I don't think you can deny either nature nor nurture.

My dad enjoyed hunting and fishing. I tried hunting and was not successful. I did go fishing with my boys when we were camping or at a cottage. Two of the three boys really enjoy fishing. This would be a case of a natural interest and ability rather than a learned behavior.

Neither Mary nor I excel in math and science. Her children's biological father did very well in math and physics. Her biological children all have very keen that math ability. This clearly is a case where we were not able to assist in the learning process for math and science, but with strong innate ability they did very well. One of the daughters has had a long career in banking, her son excelling in engineering.

Mary's mother was a teacher, Mary taught for seventeen years. Her oldest daughter went back to school as her family was raised and obtained a teaching certificate. Natural ability is seen in three generations.

Mary is gifted in many ways. Sewing for the children and herself led one daughter to do extensive sewing, now having her own business doing creative window treatments and alterations along with other sewing projects. Mary tends to keep many plates floating in the air and this daughter very much takes after her. She also possesses her mother's high energy. Is this genetic or learned behavior? Or both?

It is fascinating to watch certain abilities emerge whether they are learned or innate. Six of our seven children studied piano with private lessons. There were varying degrees of talent and there were varying degrees of investment in their time and practice. Giving permission to terminate piano lessons was an interesting process. We now hear from our children the question "When is it okay to quit?", as they interact with their children. Often we would ask the question "Is it our need for them to take piano, and do they really have talent to continue?"

12

GENEALOGY -- DO WE REALLY WANT TO KNOW?

I have been doing some genealogy work on the DeWitt family, the Bolthouse family, Mary's mother and father and some of Jan's family. We know Mary's family goes back to the 1700s because a family member wrote the Broek family history. This is a rather complete history, with many of the ancestors being ministers. Many of the details in this history are the Scriptures quoted at a person's death, and who was present at that time. My father's side of the family on the maternal side goes back several generations. My Grandma DeWitt formerly was a Bolthouse, and then VanHerynen then goes back to Yonker and Boone.

Mary's mother's family was Broek, then Yonker and Boone. Mary's Boone and my Boone were brothers. Having Dutch ancestors, the possibilities become stronger that one can find a connection.

As I have traced the family history I have learned some information that is probably better kept private than shared in a public book. Doing the math, one finds that the dates of marriage and the birth of the first child can be less than nine months. It has been said "the first child can come at any time, subsequent children take nine months".

It's Time to Clean the Basement Again

Using tools like <u>ancestry.com</u> made me aware of other family members who were also doing genealogy work. I was able to take some concrete dates and feed them into the website and then matching with other people's work, I could fill in the blanks.

My first father-in-law always said that his grandmother was an Indian squaw. Going to a family gathering after his death, I learned that was not correct, but was only a myth. I did discover that his great-grandfather Zedekiah South fought in the Civil War and that my children could trace their heritage through such organizations as the Daughters of the American Revolution.

I particularly found it interesting looking at the census records of 1910. My Grandmother DeWitt signed her name and listed two children, my father and my aunt Emma. Likewise I was able to see my Grandma Anderson's handwriting with my mother listed as their only child at home.

13

DOMINEE AND THE JAVROUX

When I was growing up the minister was referred to as the Dominee. His wife was the Javroux(Yiff frouw). In our home we were not taught the Dutch language, because as a child my father went to services in English in the morning, Dutch in the afternoon and again in English at night. He didn't want us to ever have to go to the Dutch services in the afternoon. The only Dutch word we learned was huisbezoek which was "house visitation". This meant that the minister and an elder of the church would come to your home, about once every three years, for visitation. As children we were always on our best behavior and the house was spotlessly clean. This visitation was a friendly visit where the minister and elder engaged in conversation about subjects like "What we did for fun?" Or "Did we have any questions about church?". My mother would always prepare some kind of dessert and coffee. Of course the Bible and *Church Herald* were put in a prominent place.

For some families this seemed a little intimidating. The minister and the elder were gracious and made the evening event a good memory. The minister closed the meeting with prayer, praying for each one of us by name. Only knowing a minister on Sunday, attending church, gives only one side of his or her personality. Meeting the minister in our home gave me the impression that the minister was warm and caring. This also was shown when the minister came to our home to pray with us when my grandmother died. The minister also visited us and other church members when they were in the hospital.

When I was in elementary school I went to Camp Geneva, a summer camp of the Reformed Church in America. During the week there was time for Bible study, recreation and a time for spiritual reflection. The closing activity of the week was a candle lighting ceremony where individuals could make a commitment statement. I thought I might be a minister or missionary.

As a student in the ninth grade I completed the Kuder Preference Inventory that would be used in selecting courses for high school. With the choices I made, I chose a college preparatory course of study. In 10th grade I failed Latin, so I figured that I could never be a minister, because I would likely fail Hebrew and Greek. All the way through high school and college, I had the sense that someday I would be a minister.

Ministers are expected to stand up in front of the congregation and preach a sermon. I was very shy and found speech class to be very intimidating. A whole semester of speech in high school scared me out of the ministry.

After failing Latin in high school, I went on to take Spanish and excel in that language. As mentioned in another place in this book, I was encouraged to continue to take Spanish, as I used it working in the local grocery store.

When I went to Hope College in the fall of 1961 I saw Western Theological Seminary across the street. Again the thought of being a minister was on the radar screen, but not a reality because of the cost factor. Additionally, I really did not feel called to ministry at that time. Probably the major factor in not going to seminary was my fear of being before large groups of people. A classroom of 30 students would not be overwhelming: a congregation of 100 people would be quite intimidating.

In my years as a teacher, I gained confidence in public speaking. A seven week National Defense Education Summer Institute at Knox College in Galesburg, Illinois also helped my self-confidence. I was teaching in front of fellow Spanish teachers.

In 1970 my wife Jan died of breast cancer. She had always felt very insecure and yet many people came to the visitation and her memorial service. They were very affirming of her as a person. My thought at this time was "Why don't people give flowers to the living, rather than waiting till they die?" Again my minister was very helpful to the children and me especially in setting aside time for to talk.

I think this event in my life gave me a new perspective. Rather than thinking of my own insecurities, I found it helpful to reach out to others in pain. This led to a change in focus and interest in furthering my education to become a school social worker. In 1973 I was employed as a school social worker and given the opportunity to finish a degree with some financial help. In 1974 I was graduated with a Masters in School

Social Work from the University of Michigan. I continued in that position for 20 years during which time I was also active in leading Marriage Enrichment Retreats, singing in the choir and serving as a deacon and an elder in the church.

In 1992 I saw an advertisement for the First Annual Men's Conference at the Crystal Cathedral in sunny California. I made the decision to travel alone to California to go to this conference. I had not traveled alone before, preferring to share events like this with Mary and the children. Some of the details from that conference can be found in Chapter 9 "Be Thou My Vision". At that conference I heard a distinct call to ministry. I called Mary at home saying that I would be quitting my job and going to seminary. She was not surprised.

One of the speakers at the conference was Dr. Lewis Smedes. Formerly a professor at Calvin College, he was now on staff at Fuller Theological Seminary. He grew up in Muskegon, Michigan in a family where there were not a lot of financial resources. His personal stories were interesting to me. One of his expressions was "if you're a nickel, don't try to be a dime". It comes from an old Dutch expression that you are not to think more highly of yourself then you are.

During one of his speeches, Dr. Smedes said warmly "You are accepted, you are accepted, you are accepted" and I felt very much accepted. Why is it that you sometimes it takes so long for something to sink in?

I have a very special appreciation for the ministry of Dr. Robert Schuler at the Crystal Cathedral in Garden Grove, California. In

92

1992 the size of his ministry allowed him to bring in well-known speakers for the First Annual Men's Conference. Before Rick Warren from the Saddleback church was well known, he was one of the speakers at that conference. Musician Ken Medema added meaning to what was happening throughout the weekend.

Around that time, I went to my barber for a haircut and he said my hair was falling out. I went to the dentist because I was grinding my teeth. These were all signs of stress in my life and it was time for a change. In 1993 I retired from public education and became a student at Western Theological Seminary, thinking I would take a course or two. I certainly was not pursuing a degree that required Hebrew and Greek. Again, I felt I would fail the languages.

In February of 1993, I went back to the Crystal Cathedral with a friend for Chapter 2. This only confirmed what I had learned there before. When Dr. Bill Hybels issued an invitation to make a personal commitment to Christ I walked forward to make that commitment. Even though I had been raised in the church, this was an important step in my spiritual journey.

As I walked into the sanctuary one day I asked a man in the third row if the aisle seat was "saved". He said no, but it's been "properly blessed." Later, I learned that he had been trained as a Baptist minister and was heading to the mission field in Africa, with his family.

When I was called into ministry, I told Mary that at least we didn't have to go to Africa.

When I was called to ministry in the summer of 1996 I mentioned to the senior pastor Dr. Daniel Miller, that I would prefer not to do a funeral because of several recent losses. He indicated that this was not a problem for him. In 15 years I have now participated in 100 funerals and find this to be a meaningful part of ministry.

Serving in the same church for a number of years I have been able to see children grow from kindergarten where they came forward for our children's message to graduation from high school and college and on to a career.

As a grandparent I have had the opportunity to baptize several of our grandchildren. It was very meaningful this year to see a grandson make his profession of faith in his home church. I stood next to him and remembered that I had baptized him as an infant. This was a holy moment.

Eight years ago our daughter in law invited Mary and me to be present at the birth of their youngest daughter. When our children were born, back in the 1960s and 70s fathers were confined to the "smoking room". This was to be a new experience for us. When we received a call that the baby was coming, we still had some apprehension. When we entered the room we stood along the side not sure we were ready to experience this. We looked at each other and said that this is an opportunity we did not want to miss.

We saw the baby come into the world. She was a healthy baby girl. What a holy moment! Our son cut the umbilical cord, and we were able to hold her soon after that.

About six weeks later I was able to baptize her in her home church. That also was a holy moment.

Baptism

One of the two sacraments celebrated in the Christian church is baptism. During the last 15 years several baptism ceremonies stand out as unique and special.

A

While we were in Ecuador on a mission trip, Carlos, a weaver invited our mission work group to the baptism of his son Elvis. The ceremony was held in the Otovalo Catholic Church following the last regularly scheduled Mass of the morning. Elvis was dressed in a white suit. Family and friends gathered around the front of the church to witness this event. Later in the day we were all invited to Carlos's house for chicken foot soup and a celebration cake.

B

In 1998, I was called to Holland Hospital when a little baby girl was born to parents of our church. They had been raised Catholic. The pediatrician indicated that this little girl needed heart surgery immediately at the DeVos Children's Hospital in Grand Rapids. The mother and father asked if I would baptize their daughter that morning. Being in an isolette there was no option of holding the baby in the mother's arms. I asked for a small cup and was given a paper pill container. I proceeded to baptize her in the name of the Father, the Son and the Holy Spirit. Closing with prayer I told the parents that there would be a Baptismal Certificate prepared at the church on my return to the office.

The heart surgery went very well and this girl went home after a week. She continued to grow and when she was six months old her parents asked if she could be baptized publicly. I said yes. In Reformed Theology I was taught that there is to be one baptism using water. I leaned on the side of grace and celebrated with a family. This adorable girl, when she was in third grade, put on the white robe of the acolyte and lit the candles in front of church. Now she's in high school and soon will graduate.

C

A young family from our church had twins born prematurely, thus they were at the new DeVos Children's Hospital in Grand Rapids. The one twin was very healthy and thriving. The other had breathing problems and was on a respirator. A call came to do last rites for the baby that was in distress. Again this was a Catholic family and I wanted to respect their traditions. I called a local priest to find out what to do. He indicated that if the baby had been baptized, you need not use water but just simply offer a prayer of blessing. He also told me that I was welcome to use water from the church as it was water blessed from the River Jordan. I proceeded to the hospital with a vial of water and was told he had been baptized. I prayed a blessing for this baby and he died shortly after. The family asked if I would do the committal at Taylor Cemetery. I agreed to do this the following Saturday afternoon.

Being a pastor of a non-denominational church I wanted to make sure that what I did was healing and meaningful. I called Dr. Don Bruggink and he told me to use a sprinkling of water on the grave site and to certainly use the Lord's Prayer. I read Scripture, that speaks of children "Blessed are the children, blessed are they that mourn for they shall be comforted". As I prayed many of the family made the sign of the cross and I did the same over the grave of this baby. Concluding with the Lord's Prayer one of the nieces asked if we could use the rosary. I indicated that I was not acquainted with the words but they would be welcome to lead it. They proceeded with "Hail Mary full of Grace..." For the service I wore the stole that was created by Mary's quilt group. Several members of the group are Catholic and I pointed that out to the family.

D

On Memorial Day 2005 I received a call that another baby was born At Spectrum Hospital in Grand Rapids. Lexie was born very prematurely and weighed about a pound. She was maybe seven inches long. The doctors were concerned about her ability to thrive. They also saw that there was a heart valve problem and that she would need surgery. They performed surgery on her heart which was about the size of a grape. Lexie needed 24 hour care and she was able to gain weight. During the summer she had eye surgery at University of Michigan Hospital and went home in the early fall.

On her first birthday, her parents had a party for all of the doctors and nurses who cared for Lexie. Her pastors were included in the gathering. What a joy it is to see Lexie come forward for children's message. She has a big smile on her face and her parents are especially appreciative of Pastor Dennis and all the prayers that were offered on her behalf.

14

A WORD FROM MARY

The blending of our families, we feel, was the working of the Holy Spirit. Dennis and I were both single parents with the sole purpose of raising our children alone.

I grew up in a loving, Christian family. Church and family were the basis of many activities through the years. I attended Hope College for two years and then I married a person whom I had dated for four years. We moved to Ann Arbor, Michigan so he could finish his degree. I took classes at Eastern Michigan University, working to complete an education degree. Our oldest daughter was born the following year and we moved back to Holland, where my husband would join the family construction business.

Two children and eight years later, I found myself alone. The details that led to this remain private. Suffice it to say that I felt that raising three children alone would be my future.
It had always been my desire to be a teacher. My mother had been a teacher and I saw great fulfillment in her life. I also felt it would be a good career for a single mother, as I would have the same vacations as my children.

After searching for child care for my young son who was not yet in school, I enrolled in Hope College to finish my degree. Details of the separation and divorce allowed me to finish my schooling.

I found school to be very rewarding and looked forward to its completion. During one of my classes, my professor invited me to join her at Third Reformed Church, where I had been raised, for a small group gathering on a Sunday evening. She was aware of my situation and thought I might enjoy some adult interaction.

The following week I walked into the fellowship hall where there were 10 groups forming. I was encouraged to join the group where Dennis was sitting. I heard about him from my parents, as they had witnessed this young family losing their mom. For two months we did not speak to each other as we were very busy with our young families. But we really felt that God had a plan for our lives. We spoke for the first time in November about wills and child care. We were married the following April 30.

I finished my degree and then taught nursery school for 11 years. Following that I was hired to teach kindergarten at the neighborhood school where I attended as a child.

Dennis and I are celebrating our 40th anniversary this year. One of my favorite hymns is Great Is Thy Faithfulness. I want this song sung at my funeral with gusto.

Looking over our lives together, God has indeed been faithful. God has watched over us as we together raised our family and

It's Time to Clean the Basement Again

has given us strength and grace to support each other in the many challenges of life. Someone once said to us "if you want to see God laugh, tell God what your plans are"!

Neither of us thought that we would be in ministry. This has been a most fulfilling time. When a minister is hired in the church, that person does not do it alone. It is a team effort with many ebbs and flows. God's grace is sufficient as God leads those whom God has chosen to tend to the flock.

Written by Mary Kuiper DeWitt April 6, 2011 on the eve of her 70th birthday

Writings

15

ON BECOMING A CARING PERSON

Many years ago I attended a conference in Chicago and heard Dr. George Bach speak. He was one of the participants in a conference on **"Freedom, Intimacy and Caring."** He and Laura Torbet had written a book, *A Time for Caring*, and he presented some information that has become a foundation or philosophy for my life and for many people around me. Dr. Bach discovered while writing the book that there are five elements that need to be present in order for each of us to become a caring person. These five elements are friends, models, wards, advisors and teammate. He proposed when these five categories are fully addressed, one can reach out and truly become a caring person.

These categories are: Friends, Models, Wards, Advisors and Teammate.

Friends
Dr. Bach suggested that each of us could name about five friends. These are not people who we are able to share our innermost concerns and issues with, but rather people who we can sit down and have a cup of coffee with, go bowling with, or that we can relate to, at least on a surface level.

I personally am a member of a bridge group that meets once a month. These friends have met for about 20 years and each month we catch up on what each individual is doing and on what's happening within their family. We also go to children's graduation open houses, weddings, etc. However, we do not interact much during the month, other than checking whose house is hosting for bridge and what kind of food we are to bring to the game night.

As a group we decided not to send each other Christmas cards. Instead, each month we put some money in the "wooden box." This box is opened at our Christmas gathering and that money is distributed to a worthy organization in town. Often, we have collected about $200 a year just by freely putting in our pocket change, and we are all pleased at the end of the year with our contribution to a needy cause.

Models

All of us have people that we have looked up to over the years; people whom we would want to pattern our lives after. Nationally, we look at some of our leaders and want them to be good role models and have often times been disappointed. Yet, through the years a grandparent, a boss or a teacher may be in that model category.

Certainly, all of us receive a number of messages from our grandparents. Most often their guidance is helpful. As a model my grandmother said, "Don't say *can't* before you try."
If my wife asked if I could fix the washing machine, I'd try. Fix the bike? I'd try. Eventually, I realized I couldn't do all of these things, and had to learn to say,

103

It's Time to Clean the Basement Again
"No, I can't."

My Grandmother's saying was for many years, a source of guilt and self criticism. Looking up to our models in their direction is not always helpful.

At age sixteen, I started working in a grocery store in Muskegon Heights. The owner of the store was a very gentle man, Lawrence Carl, who not only was concerned that he paid his family rent, but that he paid considerable community rent. He served on the local Chamber of Commerce board. He was a Rotarian and served on the school board. That role model showed me that it is important not only to do your job, but also to give back to the community. He was also a very good teacher and an encourager. As I was working, he would give suggestions as to what we should do to complete our work effectively. Never were we allowed to just "goof off", but always seemed to be reasonably on task.

When it came time for me to consider college, he offered me a job managing the produce department or $100 toward my tuition, which, at that time, was $700 per year. I took the $100 because I wanted to advance my standing educationally. My motivation for going to school was to get out of town, as the city was quite depressed and there didn't appear to be very many job opportunities.

Lawrence A Carl
from the *Muskegon Chronicle* Date Unknown

My boss also appreciated the fact that I was learning Spanish in high school. He would give me special bonuses, because on Saturday, many migrant families came in their trucks from neighboring farms to buy their weekly groceries. These migrant workers helped him financially, keeping his business going. The amounts of money that I received were not significant but the encouragement was especially meaningful and symbolic.

A Sunday School teacher, Herman Kruizenga, every Sunday likely said,

"When you work, you give a good day's work for a fair day's wage."

There was something within his ethic that said, "Work hard."

In the Reformed Church, this very much fit with our ethos, so that even to this day I feel I have a little person sitting on my shoulder saying,

"Don't goof off!"

This kind of role model can be very helpful. You do need, however, to be mindful not to become compulsive so that your work ethic is destructive. When it is evaluated and we look at our shadow side, this model needs to be processed and put into perspective.

Wards

Each of us needs someone or something to take care of. If we think only of ourselves, we are not able to reach out and care for others. By having wards, we are forced into a position of having to care for others. Even when we are young we practice the skill of caring for others. Practicing this habit equips us to be caring throughout our lifetime
A parent cares for children

A grandparent nurtures and supports grandchildren.

A neighbor loans a snow blower or lawnmower to someone in need.

A child waters and feeds a puppy.

Having a ward, like having a puppy, gives one "life extension."

A Sunday School teacher will consider some students her wards. A volunteer at school listening to children read has some responsibility with his/her wards.

Being a Big Brother or Big Sister is a way of developing a relationship where that child becomes a ward. In going through self-examination, it becomes valuable to know that if this is a deficit area, it is one that needs attention.

Advisors

Each of us has people we go to for information.

- An accountant at tax time each year helps manage tax information and put it all in the right perspective and each year evaluate your financial standing.
- An attorney helps to draw up a will and build other safeguards that provide a legal foundation for what an individual needs.
- A financial planner is an advisor.

As we were raising a large family, we had another couple we could go to who had children just a few years older than ours.

We would say, "Okay, tell us what's coming next."

They would give us some direction on what might be coming down the line. They became advisors to us. This was not necessarily an intimate relationship, but one where we gained information. Reading books, attending lectures, seeking information on the Internet are all ways of seeking advice, but all of us need to be able to name some people who have become our advisors.

Teammate

A teammate is someone who knows our innermost workings. This is a person who is willing to deal with conflict that arises in trying to work things out. Someone who heals our hurts, listens to our concerns, is a coach and encourager, someone who really knows us intimately. It is beautiful when teamwork can happen within marriage. I have personally been fortunate to have that in my life. After many years of marriage, if one can say that his or her spouse is a teammate, that is a true compliment. That means that when you need encouragement there is a coach there, but when you need some check and balance, that is also available within the same relationship.

Many years ago, the Rev.Dr. Robert Hoeksema said that within marriage we first learn to *like* another person. We then make a decision to share our life with that person, because there is *trust*. After the trust is built and you decide to *share* your life, many years later comes *appreciation*. Appreciation fits within a teammate relationship. If we are not married, we need to be able to find someone who becomes our teammate, someone who can help us grow and develop. Spiritually, a relationship with God is one way of enhancing the teammate relationship.

George Bach suggested these five categories listed above need to be intact if we attempt to be a caring person or a care giving person. If not we will attempt to find a person to fill an open category rather than being able to get out of our egocentric self and reach out to others. People in ministry, teaching, nursing, social work, psychology, or anywhere within the helping professions, need to seriously evaluate whether they have these categories intact and grounded in their personal life.

It is also extremely important in parenting to have your own intact person functioning, especially at the point when teenage children are being raised. If a person is not intact, they really cannot be helpful to others. It has been said that "hurting people hurt people. Parents who are hurting are not able to be fully available to their children or give their best to set boundaries, listen to them and help them to grow.

For me, the result of that Chicago conference was a personal philosophy based on Dr. Bach's principles. Like a business might have a mission statement, I adopted a parenting philosophy that became a personal hallmark for checking in on my success as a person. Dr. Bach's categories help me appreciate the people in my life and the roles they play in my spiritual journey. Through our spiritual journey, reading, prayer, devotions all help to build an intimate relationship with a supreme being. Without that relationship, it is very difficult to function.

I believe that God has directed me into ministry. I have used these categories to evaluate myself and to assist others as they become caring persons or caregivers. When one attempts to use one's own power to bring change most often that person is frustrated and tends to give up. We have all learned that the first step in recovery programs is to recognize a supreme being.

16

FINDING GOD IN QUIET

Two of the most memorable days in my life where the two days I spent in silent retreat at St. Lazares retreat house on Spring Lake. The date was February 23, 1995 continuing on to February 24.

Dr. David Register a psychologist I really respect, suggested that I had many voices in my head and that a two day silent retreat would be productive. I made the arrangements to rent a room for $25 a night. This room consisted of a bed, nightstand with a lamp and a straight back chair. I brought my own food along as it could be warmed up in the microwave in their kitchen.

St. Lazares retreat house is situated on the water in a very restful setting. This Catholic retreat house has a library, large gathering room and individual sleeping quarters. On the wall over the fireplace is a painting of the Pope, probably 8 feet high. There were a few other religious icons.

Through the years I had rarely spent time alone away from home.

I brought along with me a prayer book, and the hymnal. From the hymnal I read the words:

"When in our music God is glorified
and adoration leaves no room for pride,
it is as though the whole creation cried
Allelujah"

How often making music, we have found
a new dimension in a world of sound
as worship moved us to a more profound
Allelujah

So has the church in liturgy and song,
in faith and love through centuries of wrong
born witness to the truth and every tongue
Allelujah

And did not Jesus send us home that night
when utmost evil strove against that light
then let us say for whom he won the fight
Allelujah

Let every instrument be tuned for praise!
Let's all rejoice who have a voice to raise
and may God give us faith to sing always
Alleluia Amen

Beginning on Thursday morning I spent time reading, reflecting and being present with God. I think I was doing most talking. After lunch I took a walk outside and listened to nature around me. My focus was mostly reading Psalms. Later on Thursday afternoon I began to see a theme developing. In order to get the voices out of my head I realized I had some forgiveness work to do.

At 2:30 in the afternoon I began a letter to my children seeking forgiveness in areas where I had wronged them. That letter was nine pages long. I do not remember whether I sent them the letter or not, or whether it would be helpful to them today. I do know that it was helpful to me, and I also know that it is a treasure I will keep in a safe place.

That evening I had supper with the two priests, thus breaking my silence. I talked about being in seminary and about the journey I was on. They were very supportive and engaging in suggested books by Henry Nouwen as a resource.

After dinner I went to my room to do some reading and reflecting. At 8 PM I was too exhausted to do anymore reflection or reading and I had encountered enough silence. I went to my car and got my Walkman AM/FM radio and tuned to Blue Lake Fine Arts Station. The Faure Requiem was on the radio. I listened with different ears to the music being played. This Requiem has some wonderful music. I then went to sleep, a very deep and sound sleep.

The next morning I continued to read and meditate, praying for direction. One of the documents that came up that morning was an outline for a book I would write. Such topic as "organization and the family", "communication -- family meetings", "Legacy, how do we communicate who we are"? And finally "play/vacations". This became the foundation for writings I've done over the last 15 years for this book.

After lunch I prayed for continue direction. At 3 PM I packed up what little I had brought along and went to the Spring Lake Cemetery where my parents are buried. I had a lengthy chat with them. I asked to be forgiven of the things I had done wrong. I also indicated to them that I forgive them for what they had done to me of a negative nature, and appreciation for what they provided for me physically and emotionally. I thanked them for raising me in the church. I told them that my older brother Larry was dying of lung cancer. I told them that they had done their best with the emotional, financial and spiritual resources they had. I told them about our family, and that I was in seminary hoping to graduate in another year.

I then got in my car and turned the corner to leave when The Blue Lake Fine Arts Station was playing "*Rigaudon by Andre Compra with Organ and Orchestra*". I crumbled in tears feeling relief for some work accomplished, and for the loss I would be experiencing in the death of my brother. Larry died February 14, 1996 just a year after that conversation.

17

CAMP BRUCE

This story begins in the early 1970s when we decided to get a dog for our seven children. We traveled some distance to get a mixture of Shih Tzu, Lhasa apso, and terrier, an American Daisy dog. She was to be son Jim's Christmas present, but we had to wait until January 3rd to pick her up. When we went to the kennel, we chose a little male puppy, very cute and cuddly. The kennel owner said we could not have him, because he was the runt of the litter and would not survive in a large family. We chose a female and later had her spayed.

Every night Daisy would sleep with one of the children. With seven children there was weekly rotation. On a " DaisyDog Day" it was the child's turn to walk the dog, feed the dog, and assist with kitchen duties. This was called "special child day."

Daisy dog lived with us for 18 1/2 years, finally having to be put down because of old age.

A short time later, we did a search to find a purebred Shih Tzu, and we named him Toby. Rather than me telling the story, let Toby tell it.

TOBY

They told me I was going to camp. I thought that would be better than spending time in jail, so I agreed to go. The big people here said they needed a rest, and I had a chance to try something new. Every night at the big people's house, they would tap on the jail cell and I would be compliant and go right in. Now they were packing me up, with the jail, to go to a new place.

Susan set the rules for me when I arrived at camp. She said I could not be on the sofa, and I had to sleep near the bathroom, and we would be getting plenty of exercise. I was told there were no little people at this place, so at least I would get some rest.

This place is really quiet, except when Bruce gets on his trumpet to play revelry. That hurts my ears, so sometimes I let them know that the sound bothers me. Maybe it's just the fact that it interrupts my sleep! I also found out that these people are a lot like others I know who take care of me, except that Bruce and Susan take me for rides in their car more often than others.

When I arrived, I could tell Susan was bothered about something. She would sit at the table and work on something, but usually she would have a blank stare. I tried to get close to her, but with the rules she had, I wasn't sure how close I should get. Susan seemed sad. I heard her say that her mother was very sick, so I tried to stay close by. She would take me to the nursing home, but I usually had to stay in the car. When she came out, she would talk to Bruce about how sad she was that her mother didn't seem to be getting better. Now

I think I'm beginning to break down some walls with her. Sometimes just being close says I care and I try to comfort her best I can. She talks to me, and I try to listen.

It is warmer here than at my other nights in jail. Bruce spends time cutting wood and building fires in a wood stove. If they let me, I occasionally sleep near the fire to keep warm at night. I notice now that there is a blanket on the sofa, so I decide to sleep there also. As a guest, I have to be on good behavior. I wonder what I can do to repay their kindness and attention? It certainly is better than spending time in jail. I think my behavior is beginning to improve and they are letting me out for walks, without restraints. It must be that I am behaving, and they trust me more.

The food is about the same as when I'm at the other house, in jail. I have little variety. Sometimes I get a little variety with table scraps, but I think Bruce might get in trouble with the jail warden, so I am polite and have just a little. I probably won't try too much new food, or I will be spoiled and have trouble returning to the same boring food at the jail place.

Someone once said that life events are not accidents. It is no accident that I am at camp this week. I was here just a few days, but during that time, Susan's mother was very sick and died. I think I have to minister to her with unconditional love. The nonverbal communication here tells me it's best to listen. What is most important now is my presence. Being close and getting good eye contact seems to help. Just being here has helped Susan talk out her feelings. I've seen her relax the rules a bit, as she has been involved with her grief. I guess she just needed me to be around to help her.

As you can probably now imagine this was written by Toby a purebred Shih Tzu dog. We dropped off Toby to Bruce and

It's Time to Clean the Basement Again
Susan's home for the first time when we were on a spring vacation to Florida. They had never had a dog in their home, but being good friends they agreed to take him. We were so apprehensive, that we almost called home during the week to see how he/they were adjusting. When we returned home, they suggested that we go on vacation again, because they had so much fun

About two years later, Toby swallowed a corncob that didn't fully digest. He became sick on his seventh birthday. We took him to the vet that morning and by five o'clock that day he was very weak. We received a call at nine that evening from the vet saying that he was going to do surgery for an intestinal obstruction. A few minutes later we got another call saying Toby died on the table before being given the anesthesia. We went to the vet and cried on the shoulder of Dr.Schmidt. He agreed to bury Toby in a special location. We then had to go to Bruce and Susan's to have a good cry with them, because they had become very attached to our dog. Susan felt very responsible for his death, because they had many corncobs out for their squirrels. We also had corncobs in our neighborhood. No one knows whether he got into them at our house or theirs.

What did we learn?
When we suffer a loss, the loss represents an accumulation of many losses. I grieve for the loss of my parents, the recent death of my older brother, the death of a favorite aunt, and other ungrieved losses. When Toby died, Susan also revisited the death of her mother, because Toby was attached to the memory of that grief process. Our first dog lived 18 1/2 years

and had to be put to sleep. The expectation was that Toby would live a long life, and we were very attached to him.

It is important to properly grieve the loss of one dog before committing to another. We met with Bruce and Susan after a few weeks to decide whether or not to get another dog. We decided to proceed, thus Mary researched throughout the state to find the best breed, choosing a mixture of Shih Tzu and Lhasa apso, a "shilazo." Susan went along to make the choice with us. We agreed to the full-time care, purchase, shots, etc. and she and Bruce will do respite care so we would never have to use the "Kennel" word. The new dog was named "Muffy." Frequently we called him Toby, a sign we had not properly grieved the loss of the previous dog.

We were told that when you adopt a dog, you have to expect that you will live longer than the dog. You have to be prepared from the beginning to lose him. That caused me to detach at first from a new dog, because I didn't want to get close to him and then face losing him. Now after three years I have made the attachment, and he has won our hearts.

When your dog writes the Christmas letter, as strange as that sounds, he can say some things from a different perspective, and with a special humor. Ann Landers often receives letters about people who have the dog write the Christmas letter, and we have had some fun having the dog write ours.

People who like dogs enjoy seeing the dog at your home and interacting with him. Those who dislike dogs or previously had unhappy experiences with one prefer to stay away from them. Being a dog owner creates a special sensitivity to the needs of others, as they relate or dislike relating, to small pets

After a reasonable time passed, Bruce and Susan went along to pick out a new dog, Muffy an adorable, Shih-Tzu, Lhasa apso puppy mix. We chose the name "Muffy" and they called him "Yoda" because he looked like Yoda in the Star Wars movies.

Here is Muffy's story:
"Who is going to write the Christmas letter this year?" This is the most frequently asked question of me. Certainly they don't expect me to do it. I don't have a history nor would any-one listen to someone as inexperienced as me. I don't even have an identity, since I'm often called by the wrong name. Mary was told to spend enough time grieving the major loss of Toby, yet she said she wanted to proceed with a new exper-ience. I still see her sad at times. Recently granddaughter Sarah called to recall an experience where Toby was featured in a video. I'll have to see the video with the family's recol-lections of times pass.

Grief work is hard work and these people know intellectually about grief, because of past experiences, yet this loss seemed to have hit so much harder. Likely it was because Toby was so young and the loss was so sudden. I heard he appeared healthy on Sunday, May 16, when they took him on a boat ride on his birthday. On Monday he began to show signs of sickness. Early Tuesday morning he was taken to the vet hos-pital for emergency evaluation. The doctor did several tests including a barium x-ray. At noon he was still fairly alert, and responded to his surroundings. At 6:00 p.m., he appeared lethargic and unresponsive. A call to our home from the doc-tor at 9 p.m. indicated that Toby would need emergency sur-gery for a bowel obstruction. Within three minutes a call came cane saying Toby died before he could even be anesthet-ized. The infection was so is the severe and his body could no longer fight it. They went to the hospital to see Toby and say their final goodbyes.

Next they go to Camp Bruce to help Susan and Bruce with their grief. Toby would no longer hear those trumpet credenzas. He had just been at Camp, a place he loved to go for retreat. Now all four of those adults leaned on each other for support asking what more they could've done. What if? What if they had been more careful with his food? What if "other questions"... The greatest gift of joy he gave to them was a special bond of unconditional love that will never be forgotten. Susan had a close bond with him because he was with her during last week of her mother's illness two years ago. He had a special sense of knowing when someone was in pain and he would reach out in a sensitive, quiet and caring way.
Theological questions arise when young children die suddenly. With a lingering illness, there is some time for preparation, yet when the loss is so sudden all the questions come. When grief is shared in a large family, grief is then revisited so many more times. Later, when visiting family in Pennsylvania one of our granddaughters said "Grandpa, when you see Toby over Michigan, when you're in the airplane, show him to Grandma." A four year old doesn't understand what "heaven" is. How do you explain to a small child what it is when you don't have all the answers yourself?
Yes, we are given events like this to test our faith and to learn what we really believe. Surrounded by family and close friends we work through our grief, and move on with new life for ourselves. I guess that's where I fit in. I guess I will have to be patient, accept the fact that it will take time to heal memories, and I will never be the same as Toby. I'll do my

best to give love and affection and to try to go to the bathroom outside when they take me for a walk...

Muffy died of congestive heart failure after being sick only four days. We took him to the animal clinic where they ran tests and showed that the body was shutting down. We were heartsick because Muffy was only seven years old, much like the previous dog. He gradually just slowed down and died very peacefully. Again we are faced with the decision "do we buy another dog?"

Again we consulted with Bruce and Susan since they provided respite for previous dogs. After three months we began a quest to look for a "rescue dog." Realizing that you don't know what you're getting, we again chose a puppy and called her "Zoe."

This name beginning with "Z" confirms that she is the end of the line of dogs.

In review there have been four dogs, Daisy, Toby, Muffy and Zoe.

Each has had an individual personality and each one taught us something special.

Daisy survived a family of seven small children. Each week we had a family meeting to determine who did the various tasks around the house, designated by days. At night we hung a tag on the door of the child who was "special child" and could have Daisy sleep in his or her bedroom. It has been said that a dog becomes the bottom of the pecking order. We found that be true with this dog. Daisy survived 18 1/2 years and was able to greet our first grandchild. One day Daisy was incontinent, not her normal behavior. I took her to Dr. Schmidt to have her put to sleep. I did this totally alone without calling anyone else, and it was a huge mistake. The children did not have time to say goodbye, even though they all knew the time was near. I took charge without allowing proper grieving on their part. She was Jim's dog, and then became our dog.

Toby

Number two dog Toby was born on a farm about 5 miles  away and was a registered purebred dog. He was husky, friendly and loved to travel. He moved into our home at a time when we were "empty nesters." We traveled by motor home to visit family on vacation. Toby learned the word "antique" and would sit on the table watching us going to antique malls. We of course talked to him and told him what we're doing, and somehow he seemed to understand.

Toby was the first to go stay with Bruce and Susan and while he was there they called themselves "Camp Bruce." Bruce and Susan had never cared for a dog before, and now they have the group of about 15 come at various times.

Muffy was the result of a statewide search for a new dog. Muffy grew to be 30 pounds. We moved into a condo where the dog could  be only 20 pounds. He lived there for few months and then developed heart failure and died. At this point we thought this should be the end of the line. It has been said "having a dog gives life extension." Just being mid-60s we figured that we had time for one more dog thus again we went on a search and found Zoe, a smaller version of Muffy.

Zoe

When we went looking for a dog we were looking for a lap dog. Zoe snuggles up with us when she is not playing ball. She entertains herself by putting the ball underneath a rug and then moving the rug. She will push the ball down the stairs and then retrieve it. This goes on all day until Zoe gets tired.

Zoe will push the ball to us, we throw it and then she brings it back, pushing it with her paw to bring it closer.

18

THIS IS MY BOX

"This is my box, this is my box, I never travel without my box." "Oh little boy, oh little boy, in the first drawer is licorice, all kinds of licorice."
Amahl and the Night Visitors was performed in Muskegon in 1960. The principal actors came from New York, having played in the original television play. I was in the West Shore Symphony playing last chair cello. I vividly remember Casper, one of the wise Men singing, "This is my box, this is my box, I never travel without my box." "Oh little boy, oh little boy, in the third drawer..."

Boxes play a big part in our lives.

When my Grandma DeWitt came for Christmas one year, there was a very large box in the living room, probably 2 feet square. She began to open the package, wondering what it could be. Inside the big box was a smaller box. And so the boxes she opened successively contained smaller boxes until finally she reached the center box that contained a jewelry box, holding a new watch. Grandma DeWitt had few needs and wishes. She was probably in her mid-70s at this time and the new watch pleased her. Unwrapping all those boxed brought her pleasure.

It's Time to Clean the Basement Again

I got an e-mail recently from a church member, indicating that her husband had died and that "the boys" would be bringing their dad home for burial in Plummerville cemetery. The boys were going to bring their dad home in a motor home, leaving Texas and traveling across state lines. I wondered "Is it a big box, or little box?" Having served the church for the past 13 years, I have participated in 97 funerals, and have only seen about 10 bodies. Most of the families decided on cremation, and many times the service was held some months after the death, allowing for the family to gather at a convenient time.

I arrived at Plummerville Cemetery and found it was a big box. The widow asked me to offer the words of committal. I was not dressed for this role that day, wearing casual clothes with no socks. (I had not been asked ahead to do the words) I proceeded to do the words of committal, followed by the Freemasons doing their part, followed by a trumpeter playing taps.

Packing boxes

When one moves from one place to another, items are placed in boxes and then transported to the new location. A decision can be made before placing the items in the box whether they will be used again or not. One of the rules in our house is that if it hasn't been used for a year, it probably won't be and should be thrown away, sold, or given to someone who needs it. After three years of living in a condo, it was time again this year to shrink the boxes down.

In our basement there are several boxes: old pictures, treasures, old files, old tax returns, old slides and more old pictures. Among these boxes are the archives. One box contains memorabilia of my first wife Jan. Another contains remem-

brances of my parents. This box includes pictures, the memorial book from funerals and some letters. All of the more valuable items have been dispersed to family members. Another box contains remembrances of Aunt Ruth, including many pictures of the Anderson family. Gradually I work at shrinking the contents of these boxes down to the most significant items. While in a nursing home, Aunt Ruth had a small box with the essentials she needed - a scissors, a nail file, a safety pin, a needle, a bookmark, thread, and a small comb.
My mother in law died in the beginning of this year and she had a small box like Aunt Ruth's.

In this age of digitized pictures, I wonder how many hard copies of pictures will survive. Pictures are stored on computers, but hard drives crash and the pictures are gone. Many of the pictures contained in our archive boxes are of ancestors whose names are not on the back of the pictures. Some people sell these pictures to people who have no ancestors.

What would you want your family to keep in *your* box?

Some other thoughts on boxes:
Do we put ourselves in a box?
Do we hide from others by putting ourselves in a box?
Do we box in others?
Do we put people in boxes?
Do we put God in a box? **God's box gets bigger!**

It's Time to Clean the Basement Again

Empty boxes

To work I went the other day
   Chock full of pep and feeling gay,
Resolved that I should never fail
   One time this day to make a sale.
T'was but a few short moments when
   A little maiden scarcely ten
Came rushing in with boisterous tread,
   "I'm in a hurry ma'am" she said,
      "*Got any empty boxes?*"

   She took it, smiled, then out she fled
      To catch her school mates gone ahead.
   I sighed and waited patiently
      In hopes that sure the next would be
   A customer with cash to spend.
      And no one who would just pretend
   Alas! she comes, she sweetly smiles
   "I've something to send fifty miles,
      Got any empty boxes?"

Perplexed a bit I found a box,
   A dandy one that once held socks
I wrapped her gift, I tied it tight
   And soon she faded out of sight.
Next came a lanky colored lad
   His clothes were torn, his eyes were sad.
"Ah wants a garden and I ah needs
   Please ma'am a place to keep my seeds,
      Got any empty boxes?"
Most certainly I'd not deprive,

128

A lovely boy when he would strive,
To raise a garden by himself.

I glanced around – a little elf
Stood shyly through the door
If three years old, dancing curls so tight,
I heard the voice with real delight,
"Dot any empty boxes?"

And such a happy child to see
I smiled at her, she smiled at me,
And then she bowed her head again,
" I need another one for Ann."
She was afraid to come inside
" And Rose and Julia" she replied,
"Are waiting too." We want to keep
Them for our dollies when they sleep.
"Dot any more empty boxes?"

And soon the morning soon passed by,
It was no use, of course I'd try
A little longer persevere
From morn 'til noon 'twas all I'd hear.
Some wished them long and others square
Some wanted two or three to spare.
I gave and gave until at last
I was alarmed, unless they asked,
"Got any empty boxes?"

Reluctantly my lunch I ate

It's Time to Clean the Basement Again

Then back to work in hopes that fate
Would change the balance of the day,
Return to joy my sore dismay.
My heart stood still, for who should come,
A tall and handsome gentleman.
"We're moving to the country, Miss,
Perhaps you'll help me out with this,
***Got any empty boxes*?"**

I couldn't stand one moment more.
My pep was gone, my feet were sore.
I hadn't sold a thing worthwhile,
Nor had I strength enough to smile.
I guess we'll have to close the store.
We can't accommodate one more.
Tho't I, there's nothing else to do.
Unless they buy the contents too.
We're out of empty boxes.

Written by Aunt Ruth Anderson about 1933

19

LETTING YOUR LITTLE CHILD OUT TO PLAY

They say that the two happiest days in a sailor's life are the day he buys a boat and the day he sells the boat. A good friend of ours introduced our family to sailing. He had been

sailing for many years and enjoyed having a crew member along. Our neighbor also had a very large sailboat that he called "Elvira" named after his mother. Our children enjoyed being on those boats. One day while riding my bike to the

beach I saw an O'day Day sailer. This boat was 14 feet long and fit very nicely on a trailer. Not having much money for recreation, I went to the bank and borrowed the money. Monthly payments were very manageable and were not a burden.

It's Time to Clean the Basement Again

Frequently we went out on Lake Macatawa, with a crew of two or three children. Occasionally we would venture out to Lake Michigan on a calm day. A family trip up to a cottage on Torch Lake for a week, allowed us to do a significant amount of sailing. Since we had a small motor on the sail-boat, we could also use it for some fishing.

Many summers were spent on the water, but gradually several things happened. Because the sailboat was only 14 feet long, it was not big enough to accommodate everyone. The children were getting older and it was necessary for them to get part-time jobs in the summer, thus reducing the stronger crew members. Another consideration for the "boat" was room to store it in the driveway and the need for a third car. Thus the decision was made to sell the boat.

The selling market was not very good that year, so I put it on consignment at Tower Marine in Saugatuck and a new owner was found. The bigger the boys, the bigger the toys.

My big toy was now gone.

Sometime later I found a 1972 Red Fiat Convertible on the way to the beach. Again I went to the bank to finance the $1500, paid for the car and drove it for 14 years. Several years later I found a silver Fiat (1979) convertible for $3200, with a $500 allowance for a

1972 trade in. After six more years of driving that car, I sold it for $3500. and a "cow" painting. If you do the math, the net cost was $700 spread over 20 years plus repairs, license plates and insurance ($57 a year).

Most days I would judge the day as either "ragtop or non ragtop" day.

While driving a ragtop you sense a whole new world of olfactory delights, especially when the farmer is cleaning the barn, or there is the fresh scent of rain on the pavement. It was especially fun driving this car being 6'6" tall. Small children thought they should be able to drive the car because they were the right size for a small car.

20

"ROSTROPOVICH PLAYS SHOS-TAKOVICH. DOESN'T THAT SOUND INTERESTING?"

When I was in the fourth grade at Glendale elementary, Warner Golombeck the High School orchestra director came to our classroom and played *Hot Canary* and *The Flight of the Bumblebee* on the violin. I was truly impressed. My dad played violin in high school and still had his instrument in the basement. This began my journey with stringed instruments.

The question is often asked "How do you get to Carnegie Hall?" Practice, practice, practice. With my behavior and talent I knew I would never make it to Carnegie Hall. Orchestra became a social outlet time. As I grew, the violin shrunk, so I graduated to the cello. While in high school, working at a grocery store and earning my own money, I bought my own cello. This fine instrument had a great sound, and I did enjoy practicing. In my junior year of high school an opportunity came to play in the West Shore Symphony Orchestra. Out of 10 cellos I was last chair. For four years, I played with the West Shore Symphony under the direction of Wayne Dunlap, an accomplished musical director. One highlight was playing for *Amahl and the Night Visitors* with a New York cast for the main characters and local people for the chorus. "This is my box, this is my box, I never travel without my box" "Oh little boy, oh little boy" "in the first drawer..."

After two years of Muskegon Community College, I transferred to Hope College where my music career led me to the Chapel Choir. Thus the cello stayed home. In my senior year, I was married and did not continue in choir because the annual choir trip was to the far West and I could not afford the time or the money.

In April, 1963, I put an advertisement in the *Holland Sentinel* to sell my cello for a price of $150. One couple came on a Saturday afternoon to look at it and wondered if I would sell it for $125. I said I would be willing to come down to that price. They asked if they could take it home to show their daughter, and I could pick up their check on Monday. This couple was simply dressed, polite, but I was not sure they could afford $125 for the cello.

I went to their home on Monday and they gave me a personal check for $125. I immediately went to the bank to put it in my savings account, wanting to make sure the check was good.
During Tulip Time I watched the parade, and I saw the man who bought my cello walking down the street in very formal dress, cutaway jacket and striped pants. He was the mayor of the city of Holland, Nelson Bosman. This was quite a contrast

135

from the man who came upstairs to our apartment on that Saturday afternoon.

I have become good friends of his daughter Susan, now
Formsma. I have repeatedly asked Susan if I could buy the
cello, and she has firmly said "no."

About four years ago my children gave me a gift of cello lessons with Susan, and my wife rented a cello for three months
so I could play and practice. As long as I was playing music
with Susan the music flowed. Playing alone was not very exciting. I found a system of CD music using the Suzuki meth-
od, and that is very enjoyable. My wife and I have played pi-
ano/cello duets -- not for public consumption. I still do not
practice much, so I guess I better keep my day job. Carnegie
Hall is not even on the radar screen.

Recently a family quartet was formed with a granddaughter
playing the violin, a grandson playing the viola, another
grandson playing cello, one son playing piano and me playing
cello. One Sunday morning we played for church and accompanied a granddaughter singing a solo. That led to being asked
to play for our oldest granddaughter's wedding in June of
2010.

21

THE MOVIE

Having a blended family in our case meant that we had a boy and a girl as sophomores in high school, and a boy and a girl as a eighth grade students in middle school. This allowed us to know what was going on from a male and female perspective.

One day our 8th grade daughter came home and told my wife that they had "the movie". Mary shared this with me and said it was time for "the talk". Trained as a school social worker I had worked with students in the schools, especially working with the boys with "the movie".

I was sitting in my office doing some work and my eighth grade son came to me and asked if we could talk. I thought to myself, "This is easier than I thought it would be". I proceeded to share everything I knew about normal sexual development in males. I must've gone on for about five minutes nonstop. My son was a good listener and I was really pleased with how I handled the situation. After my lengthy monologue, I asked "is this what you want to talk about?"

My son said "No Dad, I just wanted to quit cello."

It's Time to Clean the Basement Again

"Didn't you have a movie today?" I asked.

Our son answered "it was about cancer".

What wonderful example I set. I didn't listen. I did all the talking on a topic I thought needed to be covered.
Now it was time to do some active listening.
"Can you give me more information about quitting cello?"I asked.

"This weekend we have a festival, and I'm worried that we will get a low score because of my poor playing" he replied.

What seemed to be happening was fear of failure.
"Have you talked to your orchestra director?" I inquired.

"He seems to be real uptight, and worried how we're going to do." our son said.

"You are really feeling a lot of pressure. Is there anything else bothering you?"

"No Dad, I'm just worried about Saturday."

"It is Wednesday today. How about trying this? You have two more days to practice. Do what you can to feel more confident about your cello playing. When it comes to festival time, play as confidently as you can those parts that you know well. If you have parts that you don't feel comfortable with, play softly or fake it. I would wonder if everyone is feeling the same pressure."

Saturday night came and all I heard was excitement for having placed with a first-division rating!

My son continued to play cello all the way through high school

22

IF LIFE IS A RAINBOW WHY WEAR ONLY GRAY.

I'm not sure where I read this expression, but I think it came out of the book <u>Fire in the Belly</u> by Sam Keen. For about 35 years now I've been making stained glass windows. When you work with people's lives you never know if you've accomplished something. When making a stained glass lamp it is a concrete object and can be enjoyed for a number of years.

In 1962, Kathy VandeBunte was a student at E.E. Felln junior high school where I did my student teaching from Hope College. She was in the ninth grade and I remember her well as being a good student. Ten years later I signed up for an adult education class learning how to do stained glass. Kathy was the teacher. The process for learning stained glass is fairly simple. You learn how to cut a straight line using a glass cutter, scoring the glass, and then snapping the glass apart. When you cut a curved line, you tap the underside of the glass using the handle of the glass cutter. After grinding the rough edges off, you put a piece of copper foil tape on the edge, fold it over, and then crimp the edge. Putting two pieces of glass together, you then lay a bead of solder on top of the copper foil tape, turn the piece of glass over and lay a bead of solder on the other side. Once you have soldered the entire piece, you clean the glass with soap and water, and then put a patina on the solder to make it either black or copper color. Through persistence and comparing notes with other artists I was able to grow the hobby into an avocation. Stained glass is different than other medium because there is no flexibility with the glass, and it requires very meticulously working of pieces together without large gaps. Often you are working with a frame that requires that the artwork fit properly. Once the stained glass piece is completed, light is needed to shine through and reflect the colors. A concept called "halation" occurs with the interplay of light and color. A mood presented is often of a spiritual nature.

Along with making stained glass windows, I took classes in fused glass, being able to make plates, bowls and jewelry. I still make some ear rings that sell for three dollars a pair.

Through persistence and comparing notes with other artists, I was able to grow the hobby into an avocation.

Joining the Black River Gallery with 17 other members, in the 1970s gave me the opportunity to market my craft. This experience of working with other artists helped me grow in the areas of texture and design. I also learned many marketing skills because all of us were expected to work in the cooperative, selling each other's work. The Black River Gallery was on the corner of River Avenue and Ninth Street, meaning that anyone traveling north on River Avenue would see our gallery. If I put a bird in the window of the gallery, I would receive calls from people wanting a window with birds. Whenever I displayed a window with bevels, I would get orders for cupboard doors with bevels.

In 1979, our son Jim was working at the Beachwood Inn Restaurant, when someone drove their car through the front door and destroyed the restaurant. Craig Buter from the Beechwood Inn called and asked if I could do a sign for the outside of the building in stained glass. I indicated I could. I also suggested that I could make some stained glass lamps, put some stained glass around the bar, and create bevel glass windows for their doors. All this was accomplished in a relatively short time, because they wanted to reopen the restaurant as soon as possible. This commission very much helped grow my business.

Another restaurant owner called and asked if I could create a large windmill for the center of their restaurant. I indicated I could, and also created five windows with tulips at the entrance. This project gave me the needed exposure and thus my business grew and soon other restaurants were calling for work to be done.

One of the resources that I encountered was a book entitled *The Zen of Seeing*. In this book you're taught that when a project is going well and the "Zen is flowing", it is best to keep working on the project. When the "Zen" is not flowing, you will make many mistakes and you might as well stop working on the project.

One spring I went to Naperville Illinois to learn from Dot Maddy a master teacher on painting on glass. Not having had previous experience in painting, I learned as Dot Maddy taught us how to apply paint on glass, layering the design from very light to dark, using a badger blender and firing techniques.

We were given a plastic bridge to paint fine lines with a steady hand. Her name and phone number were on a sticker, giving the opportunity to call her at home at any time. I did call her when I was stuck, and she very graciously helped me with a problem. One time I went to see Ed Hoy, the owner of the largest warehouse in the world. I asked him how Dot Maddy was doing and he said his "Wheaties get soggy every day praying for her." She had the big C, cancer. Some years later I asked if his Wheaties still got soggy, and he said with age he is eating oatmeal.

Working in ministry one works with people's lives and results are not always visible. When you make a stained glass lamp, the completion is a concrete object. I can say that I accomplished something.

When an order is taken for a stained glass window, there is a negotiation process determining the size, the colors, textures of glass to be used and finally the price. Thirty percent down begins the process with the balance due on completion. Knowing that my abilities are diminishing with age, I find it more and more difficult to work out a commissioned piece, not knowing whether it meets the standard of the customer or not. The customer is most often gracious, but there is always a tension on my part wanting to make sure the quality and design are what the customer wants. Therefore, I have made a policy to create windows for sale at the Wooden Shoe Antique Mall where the customer can decide if the piece is worth the price.

One of the biggest joys in doing stained glass has been working on theological pieces.

The project at Harlem Reformed Church was a family gift. Working with a large number of family members we were able to design a window that highlights Christ welcoming the stranger and encompassing symbols that were important to the church.

The installation at South Side Christian School was a memorial to a child that was killed in an automobile accident. The family wanted to show Christ welcoming the children. Whenever a piece required painting on glass, I thought of the spiritual journey I had traveled beginning with Dot Maddy in Naperville. When painting on glass, black paint is put on in layers, and fired between each painting. This means that a long time is invested in the process, giving time to contemplate and become one with the work. There is always the risk of paint not adhering to the glass, or the piece cracking in the kiln. Care must be used in arriving at an exact temperature or the project fails.

One of the things I've been trying to do is make art that is "one-of-a-kind". Attempting to make unique designs, cost is not always a factor. I've been able to make some millefiori ear rings that sell for $3. There is no way that these can be duplicated exactly because in many kiln firing process there is no predictability.

23

THE VASE

Imagine standing in line at the *Antiques Road Show* in Grand Rapids. The long lines indicate that many people have treasures they would like to have evaluated.

A black vase resided on the top shelf of the pier cabinet in the corner of the living room in the house where I grew up. Where did it come from? How old is it? I know that it is at least 70 years old.

Someone said that if you hold this vase up to the light and the light shines through, it is worth considerable money. Of course, I tried that several years ago; the light does not show through.

It's Time to Clean the Basement Again

The black satin paint on the background provides a backdrop for the flowers. Its flowers are a teal blue, orange, gray, purple, burgundy and a different shade of orange. The leaves are lime green. The leaves and the flowers have a roughness similar to frit. There are three seams in the vase with all three panels equal in size. The colors of this vase are multifaceted in a three-dimensional presentation. How was the vase made?

E-bay has on its webpage a very similar vase. It is labeled as a Tiffany satin vase. The bid is $35.

Often we want to put a price tag on an object. Something 70 years old usually has monetary value, yet the value assigned relates to the market, and the availability of a buyer. As a personal keepsake, at what price would I let it go?

Now that I have stood in line in Grand Rapids for half an hour, I ask myself many questions. Do I really want to know the financial value? Would knowing destroy the sentimental value? If it is of great value, do I want to insure it in case of possible theft or breakage?

Why am I so focused on this vase? Is it the most sentimental part of the home I grew up in? I think it all centers around the mystery. Where did it come from? What was the occasion?
As I'm standing in line I think of the word "primogeniture". Who should inherit this vase? The oldest, according to primogeniture, should inherit the vase. His decorating is always approved by "the decorator". My guess is this vase would go inside a cabinet so that children would not break it. He would be compliant and gracious and take this gift seriously as an obligation. After standing on line for 45 minutes I decided that

knowing the value of the vase would make no difference as to its future life. I turned around, went home and it sits on a shelf collecting dust. Now the next generation or two can continue the mystery.

24

WHO WOULD LIKE TO GO TO …?
Reaching out even farther.

This question was asked from the pulpit of Third Reformed Church by the Rev. Dr. Willis Jones. "Jersey City?" After church I talked with Mary about Jersey City and we decided to explore the options more carefully. Our church was being asked to build an apartment upstairs in a home for a church worker to live. Lodging would be at New Brunswick seminary in the dorms, without air-conditioning in July. "Well, at least it isn't Africa." We called our New Jersey friends Bob and Judy Stevenson who lived nearby to see if we could stay with them. They said "yes" enthusiastically. (Their home is air-conditioned with a swimming pool in the backyard).

We traveled to Jersey City in July 1989. The work was indeed hot, and the air was still and humid. Ed Raterink, a man who had been my third grade Sunday School teacher, told me that there was a job that needed to be done on the windows of the church. The protective glass needed to come down and be replaced. There had been a gasoline explosion some years earlier and several windows were cracked. The Tiffany original windows were covered by insurance and had been repaired professionally. The "Christian Endeavor" stained glass window still needed several repairs. I was thrilled to work on windows that were over 50 years old. I traveled into New York

City to get replacement glass, a royal blue German antique glass. While I was at the glass shop, I also bought some additional glass for other windows that were cracked.

This trip was the beginning of what was to become several years of volunteer mission work. Willis Jones planted a seed and it took root.

When Dr. Steve Stam, bilingual in Spanish, came to Third Church, he invited us to go on a trip to Chiapas Mexico. We agreed to go. We flew from Chicago to Mexico City. From there we took a plane that I believe was built in 1950 to Tuxla Gutierrez. Then we traveled by vans to San Cristobal de Las Casas.

We stayed in the missionary home overnight. The next day we went to Chamula and the Cathedral of St. John the Baptist. At 8 AM the priest said mass, and then he turned his head as the shaman set up various stations on the floor of the Cathedral. Using black chickens and candles the shaman offered healing to visitors. This is a blending of religion and witchcraft. From there we went to the village of Amatenango where we met Roberto. He ministers in his home reaching out to people who are refugees. There were no beds, only open spaces on the floor. As tall Americans we must have looked very strange to the short indigenous people. While we were there we worshiped together. Worship meant us singing something for them in English and them singing in Spanish or their native Indian dialect. We heard them sing *How Great Thou Art:* all four versus sung without printed words in front of them.

We traveled from San Cristobal de las Casas the next day, on mountainous ranges with roads that, for the most part had no guardrails. Every once in a while we would have to pull off to the side of the road to let another vehicle pass. This is the Pan-

American Highway. It is in need of considerable repair. If there are heavy rains the road washes away, and highway crews pound large stakes in the road. There is no warning that the road is washed out. Thus traveling at night is extremely treacherous because of changes in the road from one day to the next.

While we were on this road we started to smell smoke, and realized that the brakes of the Volkswagen van were on fire.

We stopped, put out the fire, and then realized our nine people could no longer travel in the van because the brakes were gone. In order to drive the van to the destination the driver needed to rely on up shifting and downshifting, using brakes only as necessary, traveling slowly. Six of us stood out on the road and flagged down a flat bed truck, and climbed on the back of the truck to go the 50 miles to Ocosingo where we were to work. After 10 minutes, it began to rain very hard and so we put a heavy tarp over ourselves to stay relatively dry. When we arrived in Ocosingo we went directly to the Hotel Marguerita, where the rooms were $11 a night and the cockroaches were large enough to put on a leash and call them by name. There was no toilet seat in the bathroom but we were promised that one would arrive "Mañana." (We never did see the toilet seat).

Our job for this trip was to dig deep holes for the foundation of the building that would become a Bible school. Using picks and shovels and a lot of muscle we began to dig where Carlos the local supervisor told us to dig. The holes were to be four feet across and six feet deep. There needed to be 12 holes like this. On Monday we started digging through clay and large rocks, digging the deepest part with a person in the hole loading the dirt into buckets.

After several days of digging, Carlos told us that we had dug in the wrong place. We were about a meter off. At that point we felt the hole was big enough to bury Carlos! Being a Christian group we prayed through our anger and started digging again. The lesson learned: Carlos thought that being Americans we would not take well to correction. He was hesitant to redirect the work because Americans seem to "know it all." As the week went on we checked in with Carlos more frequently. He also was more directive and was willing to give corrections to us.

Once the holes were dug it was time to build the foundation pillars. Forms were made, rebar cut, and cement needed to be mixed. Our first question was "where is the cement mixer?" Men from the various villages were working with us, and they knew how to make cement. We tried our way, and then watched them do their way. Their way was better and faster and much more efficient.

It's Time to Clean the Basement Again

Each night after the work was completed, and dinner eaten, we had a time of sharing and devotions. The men from the neighboring villages stood in the doorway the first night watching us. We sang a number of hymns as part of our devotions. We invited the other workers to join us in worship, and we would take turns singing in Spanish, English and Tzoltzeal Indian dialect. We often needed music song sheets to sing several verses of the hymn. They had all of the hymns memorized and could sing all the verses. *How Great Thou Art* seemed to be a favorite of theirs and ours.

At the end of our stay we had a communion service together and a time to share what we had learned. We confessed that as Americans we came with a cultural assumption that we knew what we were doing. We learned another system by listening watching, learning about their techniques. They were more efficient and worked as a team. Carlos apologized for creating extra work and asked forgiveness. I will never forget that moment of coming together, united in Christ's work. We not only worked at building a building, but worked at building relationships.

On Sunday we worshiped in a remote village. We arrived at the church in vans, the only ones who came in vehicles; everyone else walked. Breakfast was being served as we arrived... The dirt floor of the kitchen was an active scene; chickens running around, open fires with kettles, and the women preparing scrambled eggs, rice and beans.

Worship lasted three hours. The women and children sat on the right side and the men and older boys sat on the left. We stood and sang for a long time. I invited the children forward for a children's message. Our group sang some songs we had prepared in advance, in Spanish and English. Once the hour-

154

long sermon was completed we sang some more and then attendance was taken, for it was the annual census taking of the church.

We then were invited for lunch with all of the villagers. The chickens that were running in the kitchen that morning, were now our dinner. Along with the chicken we had potatoes, corn, rice and beans. The food was delicious and well prepared.

Sunday began at 7 AM, traveling over paved roads for only about a half an hour and then over rough terrain for an hour and a half. Breakfast, worship and dinner encompassed about five hours. Returning to the hotel took another two hours. We arrived at the hotel was about 5 PM; a long day, but well spent in worship and relationships. The parishioners were very grateful for our presence for they knew that we were there to work side-by-side with the villagers, and that we came with financial resources to do the building project.

One of the villagers who came to help was Juan. Back home his work was called "machete" which he used to cut down brush and sugarcane. His wages were one dollar a day. He was giving up his pay to be able to work on the Bible school project.

At the end of our stay we had a communion service together and a time to share what we had learned. We confessed that as Americans we came with a cultural assumption that we knew what we were doing. We learned another system by listening watching, learning about their techniques. They were more efficient and worked as a team. Carlos apologized for creating extra work and asked forgiveness. I will never forget that moment of coming together, united in Christ's work. We not only worked at building a building, but worked at building relationships.

From Ocosingo we traveled north to Palenque and then on to Villarreal for the flight home. Again we are on a vintage plane to Mexico City, and then Mexicana Airlines back to Chicago.

25

WHAT DOES IT COST TO GET MARRIED? A cultural shift...

On a cold blizzard day in February 1997, we embarked from Grand Rapids airport through Miami Florida for arrival in Quito Ecuador. We were traveling with a group of 25 to go to Otavalo, Ecuador about 10,000 feet above sea level.

Robin Tinholt has a store in Saugatuck, Michigan called "Otavalo" where she sells handmade sweaters, jewelry, weavings and other products from Ecuador. She told us about a family, Marco, Dalia and their daughter Anita. Anita was born with spina bifida and was unable to walk. This family lived in a home with a dirt floor and no heat. They had frequent sicknesses, and many times Anita was in the hospital with pneumonia. Marco and his family are Quichua Indian. Because of their level of income, they along with many in their village are unable to attend public schools, because they cannot afford the uniform the children wear. Indian schools are not well supported by the government and they lack basic textbooks and other materials. Marco shared a home with his parents David and Rosa. Next door was his sister Jimena. She is the principal of the school a mile away.

It's Time to Clean the Basement Again

A group from Community Church of Douglas decided to travel to Otavalo. Plastic buckets were placed at the entrances to the church for people to unload their pocket change for the children. Money was collected for school materials. Items such as chalk, erasers, scissors and crafts supplies were purchased from Debby and Company which also donated materials. One group of members gathered soccer balls and enough plastic tubing and netting to build at least two soccer goals. another couple in our group had two sons with muscular dystrophy, and knew of resources to obtain a wheelchair. This wheelchair would go to Anita.

We also went to International Aid in Grand Haven to collect vitamins, clothing, cold remedies and assorted other itemsWith most of our group, the language or culture anxiety was high. We were traveling to new territory, taking risks with it unknown.

Arriving in Quito Ecuador we were met at the airport by the entire Concha family, Marco, Dalia, Anita and David along with some cousins. We went by bus to a bed and breakfast for a good night's rest. The next day we traveled by bus to Otavalo. We crossed the equator, of course stopping to take pictures.

When we arrived at our destination, we immediately went to the Hotel Otavalo. Previously this was a convent. The furnishings were spartan and there was no central heat. We were given wool cubiertos (blankets) to stay warm at night. All meals were included in our hotel package which came to $11 a night.

The place where we were to build a home was not level, and contained a large tree. We removed the tree and deep roots. A foundation was poured so that we could start building. Construction was with large blocks that eventually would be covered with stucco.

While one crew worked on building the house, another group worked on the school building.

Classrooms were cleaned, several painted, and an artist in the group painted a mural depicting the surrounding area with mountains and a lake. Along with school supplies a member our group brought along a computer that could be used in the classroom.

Utilizing an Internet café we were able to send pictures of our progress back to the church, one of the schools and our children back home. Mary's classroom at Van Raalte School saw their teacher interacting with the children in Ecuador.
One-day Marco came to me and said, "Don Jaime, Dalia and I would like to be married in a religious ceremony." Marco and Dalia had been married in a civil ceremony. The church

would not marry them, because Marco had been divorced. Typically I will only do a wedding when I have opportunity for pre-marriage counseling. We decided to proceed with the planning. The pre-marriage counseling was interspersed with the building project and making arrangements for the wedding itself. Marco wanted a new shirt, I bought him a shirt. Marco wanted Dalia to have a new blouse and skirt. He also wished that Mary and I would stand up with them. Thus I got a new shirt and Mary and Dalia both got a new blouse and skirt, all with the native embroidery and detail. Marco also indicated that he would like to get Dalia a wedding ring, and of course why not make it a double ring ceremony. We bought two rings. "How about a gift for Dalia?" We bought a pair of earrings in the market.

Momentum grew as the members of our mission team decided that we ought to have a dinner, wedding cake and flowers. Some people made arrangements for the wedding cake and paid for it. Others bought flowers. A band was hired to play music.

We were to travel home on Friday so we set the date for the wedding as Thursday night. About 100 people gathered in the lobby of the Hotel Otavalo for the wedding. Most of the people from the village had never been in the Hotel Otavalo. Marco was born there.

What happened next was a trilingual ceremony. I conducted the service in Spanish and translated into English. Their minister translated from Spanish to Quichua Indian dialect.
Dinner was served beginning with chicken foot soup. (If you get the foot of the chicken it is a sign of good luck.) Then we

were served potatoes, chicken, assorted vegetables and then of course the wedding cake. After dinner we danced and paraded around the dining room.

Usually a minister receives a gratuity for doing a wedding. In this case we spent about $200 for clothing, rings and other assorted items that made this a very blessed event.

Before we left we were told that occasionally Quichua Indians might go on strike shutting down the entire country. Strikes are called when the Indians feel they are not being properly treated. One example of that is that only five Indians are allowed to go to the bank each day. Severe discrimination causes unrest. A strike means that the Indians lay down on the highway, making it impossible for trucks, cars and buses to travel the country. We were warned that a strike might occur and we would be stranded in Ecuador.

26

CAN YOU HEAR ME NOW?
PLEASE…

In 1996 Eric Berne wrote *Games People Play*. In his book we learned that there are several games that people use to diminish the intimacy they have with another person. Such games as *Mine is Bigger than Yours* distance us from each other and are counterproductive to having an intimate relationship. This is one way of thinking.

Many of us experience pain whenever we become close to another person and they leave or die. Significant loss tends to cause people to become very guarded in the amount of intimacy they want with another person, because, if you become close to a person and that person either dies moves away or in some way disappoints you, the pain is great. Therefore, many people create alternatives to intimacy to avoid such pain. Children who have experienced divorce in their family often have difficulty relating to a teacher or other adults in authority because they are very guarded with trusting. They have had trust, lost it, and it is difficult for them to reestablish a trusting relationship. They don't want to have to experience the pain of loss again. This is another way of thinking.

Recently, I went to a parade and saw a woman carrying a cell phone as she was watching her children marching in the parade. She was intending to observe her children and to be available to them along the parade route, but she talked on her cell phone for the majority of the time that the parade was going on. At the end of the parade, she mentioned to her son that she needed to call Grandpa. She called Grandpa, they made a connection on his answering machine, and then she continued to talk to some friends on the cell phone. All of this time, the son was looking to his mother for attention and some acknowledgement, but she was in her own world talking on the phone.

My son told me when I got a computer that the internet was a "widow maker." I understand what he means by that because one can become so absorbed in the internet that one does not interact. Additionally, music files are downloaded into the computer, generated onto a disc, then played onto an I Pod or MP3 player that again shuts out the world. I really question, now, if we are becoming isolationists and don't know how to relate to one another.

When a young person is dating and goes to see a movie with their date, the entire time spent sitting in the movie is not interactive. Non verbal communication can occur by holding hands, but they are being entertained: it is observational. Going out for a burger afterwards is interactive. Too often I observe people being entertained and not relating. I really question if our technology interferes with our ability to relate to one another. Working on a computer is a solitary activity. Listening to music on a headset is a solitary activity. Two people cannot work on the computer at the same time. Often

163

computer work isolates a person in a room or an area in the house that is, in itself, remote. Palm Pilots and computers certainly are helping us to become better organized, but with the time that we are gaining through that organization, are we really gaining more time to be intimate with one another? Our children are crying out and asking for attention.

They are saying,

"Hey,Mom!"

"Hey, Dad!"

They wear a big banner across their chest saying,

"Please pay attention to me!"

Many children are diagnosed in the schools as having an attention span problem. In my experience as a school social worker, I certainly recognized that many children do have an organic problem that causes them difficulty in concentration. Yet, by and large, a greater and increasing number of children are having difficulty relating because of the poor role models at home, or because there are so many distractions in their lives with busy and frenetic activity that create a shorter attention span.

Years past, Mom calling us to dinner meant we sat around the table and had some conversation. Now, many times for some, Mom calling kids to dinner means getting in the car and going through the drive-through restaurant and getting a Happy

Meal. If this is done in the family van, there is little opportunity for eye contact or conversation.

In chapter 13 of this book, there is information about family council. That is one of the strategies that will help in creating an environment for good verbal interchange. Additionally, being aware of how our technology substitutes for intimate relationships may help the family understand that the children are so technologically prepared that they have become relationally impaired.

Children are so technologically prepared that they have become relationally impaired.

27

DUCK, DUCK, GOOSE

A pair of Mallard ducks and a Canada goose have wintered on our pond in front of the condo. During the severe cold and freeze the ducks disappeared. "Where do ducks go?" one might ask. I've been told they go to the open water of Lake Michigan. The Canada goose has a broken wing and cannot fly. Its mate is loyal and stays with her. Now that the snow is gone the goose is standing alone and makes an extreme mess as all intake must go out.

There is a war going between the condo board trying to eliminate the goose and the residents who are feeding the goose.

We get up in the morning and either my wife or I say, "The goose is still there."

What are the choices?

Do nothing.

Kill the goose.

Lead the goose to another pond and let the fox kill it.

Enforce the "no feeding wildlife" rule.

And so life goes on. Mallard ducks continue to swim in the pond with a Canada goose with a broken wing. These are tight economic times, there is conflict in the world, there was an earthquake in Chile, and yet every day the main topic of discussion is "is the goose still there?"

Summer is coming, and so this spring we will go to Goshorn Lake where our focus becomes the white swans. As spring moves into summer there are several observances.

Are the swans back?

Did they make a nest?

How many eggs are in the nest?

How many will survive this year? Last year one out of six survived.

Why did five die last year? Was it the turtles that got them or disease?

Will Judy still feed the swans this year?

In the morning we hear the birds singing. The world is coming alive. Birds travel north to south in the fall and return in the spring. How beautiful it is to follow the rhythm of the seasons. What a gift we were given with the life of a goose with only one wing.

28

SLEDGE

In the mid-1970s Mary's great-aunt died. She never married, was successful in business, invested well and was very generous to her family. Because Mary's father was a nephew, he was included in the will. Because he died in 1973, his share went equally to his three children. What impressed us was that this aunt took 10% off the top of her estate and gave it to selected charities, the remainder was shared with her family.

What does one do with unexpected money? We had a family meeting to decide what to do. Every family has a wish list and on ours was a wish to go to Disney World in Florida. We knew that we wanted some items that were objects that would last for a lifetime. Thus we bought two chairs and an ottoman for our living room. We purchased a Harman Kardon stereo system with two fine speakers. Would there still be enough money to go to Florida? With very careful planning and negotiating we said we could do it.

Because hotels are expensive around Disney World, my brother Tom found us a cottage an hour away, north of Leesburg.

We piled all seven kids in the wood grain paneled station wagon and we were off to an adventure during spring break. We had to pack light because there wasn't much room in the car. The youngest child was six and the oldest 12 and every age in between. We had a large breakfast at home, packed sandwiches for lunch and of course everyone expected that we'd stop for gas. Everyone had to use the bathroom at the same time. Our children soon learned to synchronize bathroom needs to the availability of facilities.

Going through Atlanta, Georgia we began to hear a loud noise in the back of the car. We stopped in Macon, Georgia to have the noise checked out. We could barely read a faded sign on the front of the garage that said "Sledge's Repair." Sledge himself came out to diagnose the problem. When he got our car on the rack he said it was the axle: it needed to be replaced. Of course, we asked how much it would cost and he said the part would have to come from a junkyard. It was 10 in the morning and he said we could be on the road by one o'clock. We, of course, agreed to the repair, and figured we could still get to our destination in a reasonable time. Then the long wait began.

Since we had packed lunch, we ate lunch. That lasted 10 minutes. Someone suggested we go down the road to see Jimmy Carter's house. We of course had no transportation. At one o'clock we saw nothing happening, so I asked, "What is the timetable?" Sledge said, "We just got the part, and it won't take long." Sledge then began planting shrubs. That was not on our agenda.
A black man in a Cadillac drove up. I indicated to Sledge that it was a really pretty car. Sledge said in front of all our children "He's not a bad n…. when he's not drinking." The impatient children had their jaws on the ground, not sure what to say. Of course they looked to Mom and Dad for a reaction. Growing up in Holland, Michigan, they had not heard the

word. This was our first experience in the deep South: first, the casualness with time and then language that sounded different if not offensive.

It was time for a break and all the workers took a 20 minute break. Then they began working on the car. As the boss, Sledge never touched the car, but only directed the employees in their work.

We got on the road later in the day, so we had to stay in a motel another night, not part of our budgeted expenses.

We got up very early the next morning to arrive at Disney World when the gates opened. We parked at Goofy 23 or something like that. Packing our sandwiches, we carried them in with us, and set out to have fun. At six o'clock in the evening, I lay down on a park bench, and said I could do no more. Of course, that didn't last long, and we were all up and ready to do more, including the evening fireworks. We saw it all, and did it all. We then got in the station wagon for the trip back to the cottages. Everyone in the car was asleep except the driver.

We spent a day at the cottage just hanging out. The kids went for a swim and we all relaxed. Later we found out that there were alligators and snakes in the lake. With our Michigan license plate, the locals didn't inform us. Yankees are known to know everything.

Our final day in Orlando was spent at Sea World where we saw Shamu and performing dolphins.

The total cost for this trip excluding the new axle was $788. That computed to $16 per person, per day. That was food, lodging, entrance to Disney World and Sea World, and gas each way. We felt we were good stewards of our unexpected gift. That was of course 1978

29

SMALL GROUPS

Mary and I are part of several small groups. On the second Tuesday of the month, Mary attends a church circle meeting. When she was teaching full-time this group met at 7 AM allowing time for discussion, light refreshments and yet time for people to be able to get to work. This morning group had as many as 18 women attending every month. In the evening of the second Tuesday of the month, Mary has also started a book club where 8 to 10 women meet monthly to read and discuss a book. Many times they get a "book bag" from the library that contains all the books needed for the group at no cost. Sometimes the books are bestsellers; others are books that have a good discussion guide. The rhythm of the second Tuesday for small groups works well for Mary as she can schedule appointments for work days accordingly. Both of these groups provide intellectual stimulation, a commitment to studying material and contributing to the discussion.

On the second Friday of the month we play bridge with five other couples. Prior to our marriage Mary had played bridge for some time, so part of our prenuptial agreement was that I would learn how to play bridge. I learned and then we were invited to a duplicate bridge party where I was way over my head. These people had been playing for a long time. They knew all the conventions for playing bridge, and could keep all of the card strategies in their heads. We have been in this group now for over 25 years. All the people in the group are well-connected within the community and also well grounded spiritually. We do not all regularly attend church, but we all are invested in a church community. Once a year we have a weekend bridge retreat where we play cards Friday night and all day Saturday. We prepare our own meals and engage in lively conversation.

On Sunday evenings, Mary and I participate with a Koinonia group

KOINONIA

It's hard to believe that 30 years have gone by since there was a bulletin announcement inviting individuals to join a Koinonia group designed for couples only. Our group was formed without designating a leader. Whoever was host provided light snacks or dessert, and would prepare a lesson.

Seven couples met to organize. These included:

> Bruce and Susan- music teachers, both avid sports fans
>
> Morrie and Sylvia- merchant and his wife,
>
> Bill and Carol-an insurance agent and she a secretary- he a golfer
>
> Bill and Barb- an elementary teacher and his wife with small children, sports fans
>
> Bob and Eleanor-a religion professor and his wife; she a college piano teacher, he plays jazz
>
> Mark and Roxanne-a human resources specialist, and his wife an antique dealer

It's Time to Clean the Basement Again
Mary a nursery school teacher, and myself
at that time a school social worker

The college piano teacher, Eleanor was diagnosed with breast cancer. She had surgery to remove a cancerous growth and began chemotherapy and radiation treatments. As a group we supplied meals, visits and provided transportation for therapy. As a support to the family we would go to her children's sporting events and concerts

Our Koinonia group was meeting every three weeks on Sunday evening. Following a regular format, we would pray as a group and have some kind of Bible study. One day as a group we decided to call the elders of the church and have a laying on of hands for Eleanor's healing. Several elders of the church came as well as the members of our group, and we surrounded Eleanor with our prayers and the warmth of touch. It was this lady's prayer she would live long enough to see her youngest son graduate from high school. The chemotherapy was helping, and we all felt that she would at least reach that milestone. She was able to see her son graduate from high school. Sometime later this gifted teacher suffered a heart attack and died very unexpectedly.

One might ask if there was value in a laying on of hands with prayer. Certainly her cancer was not healed. She did get to see her son graduate. One thing that happened in the process of the prayers was that this woman was able to address a difficult relationship she had with a friend. She went to her friend to heal the differences asking for forgiveness and saying words of healing and forgiveness. The cancer was not healed, but

174

Eleanor was very much at peace. As a result of this conversation prompted by prayers surrounding this woman several months earlier, Eleanor and her friend no longer experienced hurt and separation in their friendship.

BUILDING TRUST

The organizer of our group one day suggested we take a mystery ride. When Mary and I were first married someone took us on a mystery ride to Grand Rapids. When we entered the home of the stranger back then, we sat down in a circle. The words "the American way" were written on a blackboard. I began to crawl inside myself at this new invitation and voiced the words "get me out of here." Years ago the "mystery ride" resulted in an invitation to become a dealer for Amway. When the our Koinonia host suggested a mystery ride, our past experience came to mind and Mary and I were very apprehensive yet decided to trust this event.

Getting back to the story -all seven couples gathered at a restaurant for breakfast and then traveled south to Grand Ledge, Michigan. When we arrived at the designated site we were given instructions and materials to go rappelling over the side of the ledge. The planner for this event had done this activiity several times and was very confident. Several in the group were able to trust and follow him. I had real difficulty even getting started and so did not participate.

ACCOUNTABILITY

With our Koinonia group came accountability. As mentioned in another place in this book, when I was in junior high school I had one pair of pants and two shirts. As a result, I realized that I now had an addiction to buying shirts. I will not enumerate how many I had at one time. I shared this with the group, and from time to time one of the members still will ask how I'm doing with this addiction. If I mention in the group that I have bought a new shirt, this man will ask how many I've given away. That kind of accountability is helpful to me in using restraint when I go shopping.

While raising a family there were times that I would have very controlling behavior. Dr. Lars Granberg once said "Home is the place to be, to go away from, and come back to". The teenage years are a time for children to explore letting go and while sometimes it's hard for parents to let go. I was one if those parents who had trouble letting go. One of the members of the Koinonia group helped to confront me and "buzz off". He helped me see what motivation was behind some of the teenage unique behaviors. The task of parents is to work themselves out of a job. It is a painful process for a parent as well as for the child. Yet it needs to happen and sometimes there are bumps on the road. The accountability and support of the Koinonia group helped Mary and me move through the process more smoothly.

BONDING

Our Koinonia group has gone through several stages. We have experienced the birth of children and grandchildren. We've experienced the loss through death of two of our members. As Mary and my children were married, Bruce and Susan offered to drive to the weddings and Bruce played trumpet for the brides to walk down the aisle. This meant trips to Pennsylvania near Philadelphia, Iowa, Kansas City, Missouri and the suburbs of Chicago. Bruce and Susan also were generous in paying their own way.

As careers have changed for several individuals, encouragement from the group helped ease those transitions. If one of the members was coaching soccer, members of the Koinonia group would go to a match. On occasion we would all go to Chicago, stay overnight in a hotel, go to a Cubs game and all worship together on Sunday morning. This provided very good bonding.

Mary and I launched a small group at Community Church of Douglas some years ago. That group has grown spiritually through Bible study and prayer as well as fellowship.

30

AGING AND SAGING

Many books have been written about the aging process. A friend of mine says that after age 60 you know the first names of many doctors because you move into a phase of "patch and repair". A urologist once said to me, "the work of a urologist is simple, either you can or you can't go." The aging process is not quite that simple. There are degrees of change within our bodies and our mental capacity.

About six years ago, I was diagnosed with Parkinson's disease. Mary's cousin asked me one day when I was going to see a neurologist. She noticed I was having trouble buttoning my shirt. Mary and I went together to the neurologist. He performed some very simple tests in his office and he gave the diagnosis that day. We walked out of the office and wondered what life changes we would have to make. It was not a death sentence, but it was going to have an impact on our lifestyle. I was not satisfied with the first doctor's bedside manner, so I went to another neurologist for a second opinion. The diagnosis was the same, but the treatment options seemed more realistic and more progressive.

One of Mary's first comments was "I guess you have to sell the convertible". My response was "I bought the convertible;

I'll decide when to sell it". I had driven a Fiat convertible for 20 years and I wasn't quite ready to give it up. I drove the car about two more years. Both Mary and I would have a contest to see who could get in or out of the car the easiest. Finally we both were having difficulty, since the car was so low to the ground.

When the diagnosis came I had many questions, primarily, "Is this a genetic disease?" I suspect my father had Parkinson's, he also had arthritis. He only lived to be 68, so it's hard to say what his diagnosis was. I recall that he had many of the symptoms. My children are asking if it's genetic, and what can be done to prevent the progress of the disease. There is no cure, but I have found several things to be very helpful:

- I get a therapeutic massage every two weeks year round. I've been doing this for 15 years. When I went the first time, I thought it was decadent, but soon decided it was essential. Good therapeutic massage helps to rid the body of toxins. It very much helps me with arthritis symptoms. I go to a masseuse who prays before she starts, and only engages in verbal conversation when I start a conversation. She is very respectful of my need for space and quiet.

- I learned that regular exercise does make a difference. I notice when I haven't been exercising. I find two or three days a week restorative. I use an exercise bike to go about 30 minutes at a fast pace. There's some evidence that this helps the brain activity and especially is good for patients with Parkinson's. Getting the RPMs up is essential. This of course releases endorphins that are very helpful to our well-being. Physically it cannot replace the dopamine that is lost in Parkinson's, but I find it helpful for balance and general well-being.

- Good nutrition is essential. As much as possible our cooking is done from scratch, being very careful not to use artificial colors or preservatives, buying fresh whenever possible.

- When I have times where I'm not as functional, I see a look on people's faces that says "oh that poor man" or "he looks drunk". Medication is helping my condition, but there are times that it's "on" and other times it's "off". With my flexible schedule, I am pretty much able to regulate the "on" times.

- In chapter 6 I indicate that we have a number of small groups. When we play bridge in our group I begin the evening able to shuffle and deal cards. As the evening progresses my eye/ hand coordination diminishes, and someone at the table is willing to shuffle or deal for me. This group has realized that I like to do as much as I can, but I'm willing to ask for help.

- Mary has learned to relax around me, realizing that this disease process is a long haul. Initially there was "shock" and some uneasiness and protectiveness. Our kids would call once in a while and ask if Dad has been "grounded". This is especially true when there is ice on the ground and both Mary and I are fearful of falling. When Mary was gone out of town for a few days, she wanted to make sure that there was someone available, in case of emergency. If we go to the mall shopping, and I get tired, she will say "Sit and stay". I respond appropriately and jokingly say "Yes dear".

- Humor is helpful at times. Even though I don't have much of a tremor, I say that Parkinson's makes me "a mover and shaker". When someone asks "How are you doing?" I will many times say "about 6" or "about 9 1/2". Sometimes I will jokingly say "about 2". The response I get is "is that if a scale of five or 10?" My response is "You choose".

- I have heard that 50% of the people with Parkinson's have dementia. I'm not sure if it is related to the disease or to normal aging. One thing I have learned is to remain mentally active. Sitting in a chair and "vegging" is not an option. I strive to learn something new every day. It might also be a new technique for doing stained glass. It might also be learning a new computer shortcut. Reading a historical novel helps to keep the mind active. Taking a class uses brain cells. Teaching a class gives an opportunity for logical planning. It also becomes a goal that can be accomplished.

31

DO OVER'S

As one reflects back on his life, there are probably some regrets along the way.

In 1962, my wife Jan and I were given a 1954 Dodge two-door sedan as a wedding gift. It cost my in-laws $200 and we knew its history. This car had received excellent care and the mileage was accurate at 54,000 miles. It was silver gray and did not show dirt. The Dodge was a stick shift and got excellent gas mileage. This car was dependable. Living near the school where I taught, we needed only one car as I was able to walk to work each day.

As men do, one day I got an itch for a different car. The muffler was starting to make noise and I felt we needed a different car. I shopped many car dealers and settled at one that had a 1959 Plymouth four-door sedan. By this time we were putting child car seats in the back seat and a four-door car seemed to be a good decision. This cream colored Plymouth seemed to be a good buy. It had 85,000 miles and appeared very well cared for. I struck a deal and drove away in a car with an automatic transmission.

When I arrived at school next day (of course I had to drive the car to school to show it off) one of the seasoned teachers said he thought that I had just bought his car. He said it was a honey of a car and gave him good service. He also said that he traded it in because it had 149,000 miles on it. Here comes the do over part. I was too naïve and too shy to go back to the dealer and confront him on the mileage differential.

To this day when I drive past that car dealership I have some feelings. One, I think the dealer did an illegal act by changing the mileage. If not illegal, then certainly it is unethical. The second feeling I get is regret for not confronting the dealer. Finally, I feel it's time to let go, and that's the hard part. I don't like people taking advantage of me, yet I need to let it go.

I've often said that a person does the best he can in a situation, based on intellectual, emotional and financial capabilities. This became a first step in the learning process where I became more assertive. Lessons learned become a way of life. Despite my wish to do over, the car met my original expectations.

Many years ago, I was invited to teach the Hope College class *Exceptional Child* a special education course required for education students. When I was a student at Hope College back in the 60s, all the instruction was lecture. Obtaining a master's degree in social work, and working in special education as a school social worker, gave me the qualifications to be a part-time instructor. Not knowing better at the time I conducted my classes primarily as lectures with written exams following the teacher manual suggestions. Topics such as visual impairments, hearing impairments and learning disabilities were covered during the semester. Students who overall did well academically, excelled in the class. Students who had some learning style difficulties did not do as well.

When I was a college student, I did not do well with the format of lecture, taking notes, and reproducing information in a multiple-choice test. Now I was teaching a class using the format in which I had done poorly. As a graduate student I was given projects and I succeeded in doing those projects with excellent grades. Looking back now, I wish that I would have structured the class to meet the learning styles of the class members. Not only did I teach the class once, I was invited to come back again while the regular instructor was on sabbatical leave and again I used lecture format. I would certainly do things quite differently today.

On a rainy day in Florida about 15 years ago we were walking in the mall and a sign said "free trip to the Bahamas." We had nothing else to do that day, so we sat through a presentation on "vacation opportunities." Mary and I were both working, we enjoy travel and we decided to purchase a "vacation opportunity." One week in Miami Beach looked very good in February. We were told that lots of people want to spend time in North Miami Beach, and we would never have to worry about getting a room to our liking. We signed the papers and now have a deeded property at the Westgate Time-Share Resort. Our maintenance fee the first year was reasonable, and it seemed like a good deal. However each year the maintenance fee goes up, and now we would like to be free from that responsibility.

We have written on our forehead "sucker." There is no market for used timeshares. We are stuck and we know it.

32

OOPS

I often say that a person does their best, with their physical, emotional, financial and spiritual being. I guess I believe in the goodness of people. I know that some people set out to do wrong because of deviant ideals. Generally I feel at any given time that I'm doing the best I can given the current resource. So why am I writing a chapter called *OOPS*?

In the previous chapter I wrote about *DO OVER*". Looking back I would like to have been able to do some things over again, but I did learn from those experiences. Subsequently I have recalled other situations that I would like to do over.

Failing Latin in high school still remains with me. I don't think I could do it over again, remembering how difficult it was at that time. Developmentally I was not mature enough to be disciplined to study declining verbs. Spanish was more fitting to my intellectual ability, and I did also not want to fail a second language. I believe that failing Latin was the motivator for me to succeed in learning Spanish. I remember the expression speaking of Latin "First it killed the Romans, now it's killing me".

Setting the bar of achievement high can be a motivator. Setting the bar too high and unrealistic can cause pain when goals are not reached.

It's Time to Clean the Basement Again

As I stated earlier I did not pursue a Master of Divinity (M.-Div.) degree at Western Theological Seminary because I was fearful of failing Hebrew and Greek. I thought also that an M.Div. degree would lead me into ministry that would require preaching regularly. I thought my focus would be counseling, working in a large church and having weekends free to travel. God had another plan. I was called to Community Church of Douglas as an associate pastor with the understanding that I would use my gifts inf calling, counseling, assisting in worship and occasionally preaching as needed. This seemed like a good fit as I really do enjoy those areas of ministry. I even volunteered to preach a sermon that went quite well. I have even gotten to the point where I have enjoyed preaching. Several times I was called to preach at the last minute because of emergencies that arose with the senior pastor, such as sickness or the death of his father.

I would say that I have overcome a considerable amount of fear of failure. God has helped me overcome that fear.

I felt a nudge to complete a M.Div. degree, but still had that fear of failure looming in my head. I consulted with the Holland Classis of the Reformed Church in America(RCA) and was directed to the Approved Alternate Route of MFCA (the Ministerial Formation Coordinating Agency.)

I then pursued a program of study that would lead to ordination in the Reformed Church in America. I took courses and passed them. I did projects and passed them. I took a preaching class at the Crystal Cathedral and passed it very comfortably.

Once my course work was completed it was time for Classis exams. I met with the seminary seniors to get a preview of what might be asked. I sat there feeling very inadequate, but decided to persevere. On the night of the exams I sat in front of the gathered body and questions were asked in rotation. When the questioner presented my question it was "Does the Reformed Church belief in regeneration in baptism"? My answer was "Yes". When the questioning was over all the students were asked to leave the room and await the results. When I returned to the sanctuary I was told that I did not pass. I was stunned, but aware that there were many gaps in my learning. Was it time to quit? I was embarrassed and discouraged.

The Rev. Dr. Larry Schuyler, Classis Coordinator encouraged me to keep going and so I spent another year of study. I took more courses, studied new material and went back to the MFCA board for another evaluation. They were gracious and I passed. Again I had to go to the Holland Classis for an exam. They changed the format so that I didn't compete with seminary seniors and I passed. I grew from this experience, and I know I needed the extra year to complete some more coursework. Perseverance paid off. At age 63 I was ordained as a minister in the Reformed Church in America.

As Dr. Lars Granberg said once "Home is the place to be, to go away from and come back to" I had been a member of the Reformed Church in America for many years. I then served a non- denominational church. Now being back home in the Reformed Church I actually have two homes as I continue to serve Community Church of Douglas.

People

33

JANNA HOLLY SOUTH

Janna Holly South was born on January 3, 1943 in a home in Muskegon where babies were birthed and raised in Muskegon Heights. The family lived in a rental home at 1035 on Howden Street. When she was maybe 2 1/2 years old her parents bought a home at 520 Howden for $3,500. Later the address was changed to 2021 so the numbers would coincide with Muskegon numbers across the tracks. The cities began to work together a bit.

Jan was the youngest in the family, Vern being the oldest, then Avis, and Bobby, who died at age 5 of diphtheria, then Larry. She attended Lindbergh school across the street from the church that she was raised in, Covenant Reformed Church. Jan's dad worked at Wolverine Express as a traffic controller, working in the office a number of years. Her mother worked at Hilts in the paint and wallpaper department, thus when it came time to decorate there was always a discount on paint or wallpaper.

The family moved from Muskegon Heights in 1956 to Fortenbaker subdivision, where Jan would take the bus to school or get a ride with her dad. Her sisters lived at 2324 5th Sreet for almost 2 years, so Jan would go over and hang out with Avis sometimes and would be picked up there when Dad got out of work.

It's Time to Clean the Basement Again

Her parents sang in the choir so after church or choir rehearsal they would go out for dessert with Sam and Emma Work-
man. They became very good friends. At times the Souths and
Workmans would be a quartet.

In high school Janna was very social with several girls including June Graham (her dad called her graham cracker), Karen
and Skip Hughes and many others. She enrolled in classes that
had a secretarial theme and she was very good at shorthand,
typing and bookkeeping. Choir was always a part of the mixture. The youth group at church was called *Christian Endeavor*, an organization known nationwide for helping adoles-
cents grow spiritually. *Christian Endeavor* was an RCA youth
group. They gathered in the church, but also attended classes
and presented hymn singing events. Jan's parents, mother
from Vriesland Reformed and father from Forest Grove Reformed met at a *Christian Endeavor* gathering and later were
married.

My parents, the Souths and the Workmans got together quite
often for coffee.

Jan and I started dating when I was a high school senior and
we went to the prom together. In the fall of 1959 I went to
Muskegon Community College with Janna being two years
younger. In the fall of 1961 I attended Hope College as a juni-
or and Jan was a freshman.

Pretty early in her freshman year one of the teachers told her
that her sister would have answered a question differently.
She lived with a lot of personal insecurity and having an older
sister who was quite successful academically became difficult

for her. Her high school training was mostly in secretarial courses so many of the college courses were difficult. Jan finished her freshman year with a plan to work the next year rather than continuing in school.

That spring we were dating very seriously and we sat down with our parents and indicated that we want to get married. We would both work during the summer and save money for tuition for my senior year. Jan worked at Wolverine Express and I worked at Highland Park Dairy stacking milk crates. We were married on September 5, 1962 at Covenant Reformed Church.

In the fall we rented an apartment over the Holland Theater for $50 a month. We were given a 54 Dodge sedan as a wedding present (worth $200). That car served us very well.

I remember one day going to Van Hemerts to buy a used television for five dollars.

Jan worked at Jack's restaurant on 8th Street across from the Civic Center. I worked part-time making picnic tables for Sears. By November, we realized that Jan was pregnant and so we worked with a doctor for prenatal care. I remember one night putting chains on the tires because we'd had so much snow that we needed chains to be able to get to the doctor's office.

I graduated from Hope College in June 1963 and Mark was born in July. The summer before I started teaching at West Ottawa I worked at Vans Pines for a $1.25 an hour and then went to the Blueberry Growers Association for a dollar an hour, but working 80 hour weeks.

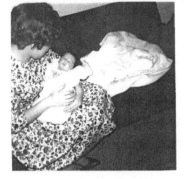

Rent for a duplex on Franklin Street was $90 a month. We did well with one car because I could walk to school. Our landlords was Lee and Linda DeVisser. We were able to borrow $500 from my parents as a down payment on a house at 390 W. Maerose. We did the painting and staining with material bought at Hilts. One of the things we did was use a water-based stain on the cupboards and trim. It made for a lush cherry finish. The bedrooms were adequate and we finished off the lower-level as a family room.

Mary Kristin was born in January of 1970 and the doctor indicated that the swelling underneath Janna's arm was an auxiliary mammary gland. In April of that year she had surgery that was defined as a biopsy. The doctor came out as I was sitting alone and told me that they had removed the breast and that it was likely cancerous. I felt I had no warning and Jan was not prepared for such drastic surgery

.

Because she was young, there was a feeling that cancer would spread rapidly so they scheduled an additional surgery to remove the ovaries. This was done in early May. While they were in surgery they discovered that the cancer had metastasized, spread to the liver and had probably spread to other portions of the body. Jan began chemotherapy, which really wiped her out. She lost her hair and wore a wig that looked very much like her natural hair. During the summer I was working for the Michigan Department of Education in migrant education so one of the Boelkins girls babysat so I could go to work.

At this time in history there was no organization like Reach to Recovery, or Hospice. The lady at the drugstore where Jan was fitted for prosthesis was very helpful.

For the most part Jan was able to function quite well considering what she had gone through. She had energy to care for the children. The cancer had spread quite extensively so that the chemotherapy at that time was not very successful. She was able to go to the West Ottawa High School prom in June of 1970 as a last outing.

During that summer many people of the choir brought in food and offered to babysit.

One day Janna fell in the kitchen and was taken to the hospital. After 10 days in a coma, Jan died on August 19, 1970. Her funeral was held at Third Reformed Church in Holland with the Rev. Mark Walvoord leading the worship. Roger Rietberg played the organ and an ensemble of women sang. (Jan sang in the choir as long as she was able to).
  Mark Walvoord was young, but showed real depth in working with our family. He went to the library at Western Theological Seminary to find materials for me on how to talk to children about death and dying. One of the things I recall was that it was important to tell children about the finality of death. That going to heaven wasn't just walking up the stairs, because if you walk up the stairs, you can come back down the stairs.

It's Time to Clean the Basement Again

The theme for Mark's sermon was "Why?" Many years later I was asked if I knew the answer to the "why?" It is my belief that we are given the question is a gift, giving us the opportunity to struggle with the question. If answers are given to quickly we do not wrestle with the questions. I have been given the opportunity to grow considerably as a result of this passage of life.

Two weeks after Jan's funeral it was time to go back to work teaching at West Ottawa. The mother of one of the teachers became a babysitter, but then I discovered her eyesight was so poor that she could not find pins on the floor and I had to let her go. Mary Kristen was eight months old, Karen three, Jim five and Mark seven years. My parents paid for Jim to go to nursery school). The next babysitter had back trouble, and also had to be let go. My parents came down for two weeks driving from Muskegon each day. My dad had retired from the dairy so he was available, but this was not a long-term solution.

I discovered that Gracie Nagel the wife of a seminary student from Canada was looking for work, and could not earn anything under Social Security. I paid her $45 a week cash. She cared for the children very well, was very organized and was able to write letters in the afternoon when the children were sleeping.

34

GRANDMA DEWITT

The thing I remember most about my Grandmother DeWitt was that she frequently wore navy with a white pearl necklace and white pearl earrings. She was widowed at a young age. The 1910 census shows only two of her three children. My Grandpa Harry DeWitt died of pneumonia when my dad was two years old. Younger brother Cornelius (Red) was only a baby and our dad was sent to Spring Lake to be raised by Adrian and Nell Bolthouse. Dad returned to Muskegon Heights to graduate from high school.

Grandma was known as a very quiet, stoic woman. When Grandpa DeWitt died, he left a widow with small children and the business that he was running called Buckley Hardware

195

It's Time to Clean the Basement Again
located between Carl's grocery store and Parsons department store.

Buckley hardware store

Grandma DeWitt, Dad, Emma, Red on Grandma's lap.

Many people owed the family money and so Grandma was known for going into the bars on Friday to collect money that was owed the family, before the men had a chance to drink up their paychecks. In later years she worked at the VandeVelde Furniture Company. The small green rocking chair in our basement family room was a gift from Grandma DeWitt when I was five years old.

When Sam and Emma were married they made an apartment for Grandma DeWitt in the front of the house on Jefferson Street. She had a bedroom and a living area and joined them in the kitchen for meals. Emma taught piano lessons, played piano for church and accompanied Sam as he sang solos in various churches; both Sam and Emma sang in the choir. Sam and Emma never had children but became a special aunt and uncle to our family boys and to Dick and Dave, Red's sons.
Every Wednesday Grandma DeWitt would be at our home for dinner, because Sam and Emma went to choir rehearsal. We had a radio with a large speaker and every week we listened to *Ted Mack and the Original Amateur Hour*.

One day Sam and Emma and Grandma DeWitt sat down and decided to "take down the wall". They remodeled the home to be more open with a living room area in the front and the dining room.

In 1952 Sam and Emma decided to buy the home from Emma's brothers.

My parents bought a 1952 new black Nash Ambassador. This was the only new car we knew.

Sam always drove Buick Roadmaster cars, the four hole on the side, "big Buick." They had an Irish setter dog. I always remember Sam smoking a pipe.

Sam worked for March Irrigation building sprinklers for large farms. After a few years there he decided to start his own sprinkler business called "Little Red Jet Sprinkler." He invented this about the same time that the Melnor sprinkler came on the market. That sold for a few dollars and Sam's was over $20. My cousin Dave and I worked for Sam, milling some parts part-time. The sprinkler had four wheels and an arm that went back and forth, with a piston that had leathers that had to be replaced. This was sprinkler that needed a lot of maintenance, so Sam kept busy with repairs. After it became apparent that the sprinkler would not support his family Sam took a job at Bennett Pump in Muskegon Heights.

Emma never worked outside the home. Because Sam and Emma lived just around the corner, I would go over and talk with them frequently because they were good listeners and engaged in conversation very well. I would get scolded from my parents for "airing the family wash." Most often we sat on the back porch with these conversations.

When it was strawberry season, Sam and Emma would have strawberry shortcake as their entire meal. Again, when corn was in season that also would be their entire meal.

Emma packed a lunch for Sam every day with a thermos and sandwiches and something homemade.

Emma had considerable bronchial problems through years with frequent colds and coughing. She died of cancer at home, cared for with hospice and Sam very attentive to her needs.

One year Sam, Red and my dad bought a Chris Craft kit boat that they put together from scratch. The deck was mahogany, and I remember soaking the wooden boards in the bathtub and then bending them in the doorway, allowing them to dry so that they formed the hull of the boat. This was always referred to "Red's boat. He started and maintained it, but we got to use it during the one-week vacation we had at Big Blue Lake. The boat was not fast because I think we had only a 5 horsepower motor on the back of it. Thus it was not used for waterskiing or any recreational sports other than fishing.

I remember my dad coming home from work one day and my mother greeting him on the back steps saying "Your mother is changing colors." This came to mean that she was dying. Being quite young when she died, I don't have many recollections of her other than those mentioned earlier. I think my dad inherited his quietness from her.

35

MOTHER KUIPER – MARY'S MOM

Alma W. Cook Kuiper was born on Oct. 31, 1911. She was the youngest of four children. Alma's family was well educated. Her father was a family doctor and her grandfather was the third minister of Third Reformed Church in Holland. Alma grew up at 34 East 14th street. .
She attended the Holland schools and graduated from Hope College in 1933.

She taught 3rd and 4th grade in Grand Rapids, Michigan. for three years, while living with an aunt and riding the bus to work each day. She then came back to Holland and taught at Lincoln school before her marriage to our dad Chester Kuiper. Together they started their marriage at 195 West 20th street. Grandma Cook moved in with them shortly after and had her own apartment upstairs

Chet and Alma joined Third Church and Dad served on consistory both as elder and deacon. Many Sunday nights were spent counting the day's revenue with close friends.

Dad's health declined at a very young age. He soon became victim to the "family" heart disease and had a major heart attack at the age of 37. Life became one of many hardships thereafter. Now with a young family of three children, Mary age 8 years, Ruth age 5 and Paul age 2, Mother had to nurse Dad back to health and manage her family.

Dad returned to work and managed the Temple Furniture Company. Frequent business trips took him away from family, but mom managed to keep us all going. She was a doting mother and always supportive of our endeavors. She made many sacrifices on our behalf. She lovingly nursed us through childhood diseases of scarlet fever, measles, and chicken pox. We see now that her excessive worrying was just an expression of her deep and abiding love for her family.

At age 50, Dad suffered another heart attack and also closed the furniture business. He became a stockbroker and worked for Buys and MacGregor. Mom went back to the classroom again and was hired to teach Kindergarten at Pine Creek School in the West Ottawa System. She loved this job and many parents were so happy to have her as their child's first teacher.

During the years of 1971-1973, Mom suffered some significant losses. Her beloved sister, Edna Wyngarden died of breast cancer, brother Herbert died of heart disease and Dad suffered

It's Time to Clean the Basement Again

a fatal stroke in 1973. While stents, open heart surgery and drugs were not available for Dad, Dr. John Winter said Mom kept Dad alive for 20 years with her careful attention to diet and lifestyle. Mom taught for 2 more years after dad's death, then retired in June 1975.

Her life was now to be centered on children and grandchildren. She was the cookie grandma to many kids, often baking for their many events. Mom's steady faith kept her going in spite of missing loved ones so much. She often was an example to all of us for her spirit and belief that God was in charge.

We as children have often wondered why mom lived so long. She lived longer as a widow that as a married woman. Leaving her home at age 89 was difficult, but she soon adjusted to her new environments. Resthaven Care Center and Oak Crest Manor were supportive and loving places for her. We feel blessed by the care given to Mom by Third Church members and pastors.. Mom's journey is now over. She is now home with her Lord and those whom she missed so much.

Written by Mary Kuiper DeWitt January 2010

35

AUNT TRINKETS

Aunt Ruth Anderson Klett was a special lady. She was gracious, kind, patient, loving, hard-working and sensitive. We would never consider calling her "Aunt Trinkets". A friend of ours coined the word after hearing about the events in her story.

On a cold wintry day we called Aunt Ruth to see how she was doing. It had been a long winter, and her driveway was rarely plowed, so she was sitting home alone. Neighbors would bring in groceries. Before Christmas the snow had started and she found an old piece of hardinger lace. That became our Christmas present that year as she added a couple inches of crocheted lace around the original piece. That continues to be a treasure in our home.

My wife Mary said:"Don't you think it's time to move off the farm?" Aunt Ruth was 78 years old, living alone on limited income. The house stood on five acres and was in saleable condition. "Yes I think it's time to move." Thus the journey began.

Aunt Ruth was a collector of vases -- at least 250 two of them. Each one had a story. Where did it come from? Who gave it to her? Who was present at the party? What year was it? What event was it? Wrapping the vases carefully, listening to the stories, determining which ones moved with her, which ones to give away, all became part of that spring. Now is time for a garage sale. Again more stories.

Aunt Ruth was born and raised on a farm. The original house burned down in the 1930s and her father along with some help build a new home. Many of the furnishings of that home came from friends and family in the 1930s. Trunks of clothing were sent from Milwaukee. Those old trunks now antiques, went to family. Moving from a home to an apartment requires a lot of shrinkage. A move is not only physical, but strongly emotional. Ruth had stayed home to care for her parents, never married, and worked at Parsons Department Store for over 45 years. Every Sunday she drove to church, usually with children that she would take to Sunday school. Wednesday night prayer meetings were also part of her schedule. Friday nights the store was open until 9 PM. There was a rhythm to her week, between work and church. Church always involved worship, and Ruth leading the singing. Often she sang solos, directed the choir and directed the music during worship. Her old upright piano then naturally was given to the church.
Ruth and I explored several opportunities for apartments. She chose one within a few miles of her church. The price looked good, the house was sold, and she had enough resources to pay the costs. On moving day several pitched in to move the furniture, her bed and dresser, and about 200 vases. A new cabinet was purchased for the vases along with a sofa sleeper and the new chair and ottoman.
While on the farm, Ruth was very pleased to be able to prepare a dinner for our family - all nine of us. Dinner would in-

clude two meats that you could cut with a fork, two vegetables, salad, relishes and of course homemade pie or cake with ice cream, again two choices. Dinner was always served on the Franciscan Desert Rose dishes with a tablecloth and hand crocheted cloth napkins.

When Ruth moved to the apartment she again wanted to entertain with dinner for the entire family. That would mean 10 for dinner. The second time we were invited for dinner there were 11 of us. Ruth's good friend Carl joined us for dinner. He had been married for over 60 years, and then his wife died. He had known Ruth for many years. Carl's sons attended Sunday School with Ruth as their teacher.

During dinner we realized that this was more than just a friendship. Carl asked for Ruth's hand in marriage. The date was set for November 12 of that year. That was my mother's birthday and she was asked to stand up for her sister. I was asked to walk her down the aisle. What a joy that was to walk a 78-year-old woman down the aisle. That evening she gained two sons and their spouses, grandchildren and great-grandchildren. Moving into Carl's house meant packing things up and dispersing a few vases. The count was now down 150.

This joyful life lasted for five years. Church was a regular part of their life along with substantial family interaction. By combining their incomes, they were able to be eating out more frequently.

Carl's heart condition began to deteriorate and he died with Ruth caring for him at home.

It was time to move again to an apartment. Packing the vases and furniture was easier than the original move, and again several items were dispersed to other people. The count of vases was under 100. This move put her closer to her new family and they were very devoted to her care. One day we received a call that she had broken a hip, which involved surgery, therapy and a short stay in the nursing home. Somewhat slowed down, she returned to the apartment, but realized that she needed some assistance in preparing meals and some supportive care. The Hume Home was a location that fit her needs. The cost was reasonable, she could keep her car, and all meals were supplied. Again it was time to shrink the furniture and vases to a location that was one room as a studio apartment. This became a home for her for quite a time.

While at this location Aunt Ruth turned 90 and I asked her to write the Anderson family history. This was a real treasure and remarkably accurate, despite her age. The only error we know of is the account of her brother's single marriage: we know that he had three wives.

In time Aunt Ruth gave up driving. A hospital stay determined that she needed to go to a nursing home. Brooke Haven on Apple Avenue in Muskegon became her home until she died at age 92 in the fall of 1995. When most people have lived this long, most of their friends and family are gone. Because Ruth invested in so many children and brought them to Sunday School, there was a large crowd at her funeral.

Aunt Ruth showed Christ-like behavior in her everyday life, and in relationship with all she met. She never knew I was called to serve a church as a minister, but she said "Denny, I always knew that you would someday be a minister."

The vases have found new homes and with them the stories go on to future generations.

Editors note:

The last part of this book contains the history of the Anderson family written by Ruth Anderson Klett when she was ninety years old. She hand wrote all of the pages and then they were transcribed. This family history is a "clean" story and some of the details were sanitized. Rather than being the story of her brothers and sisters, it really is a story of Ruth and how she interacted with her brothers and sisters. She was very young when the oldest went off to the service.

A few generalizations can be drawn from this history. The men, Alfred, Joe and Rudin all served in the Navy. The women of the family worked in the homes of "well-to-do" families and boarded with those families.

Music was also part of the heritage. All the family had good voices and many of them used their voices in church

APPENDIX

The Anderson Family History

Written by Ruth Anderson Klett

1

GRAMPA ANDERSON

Augustinus Anderson was born to Andreas and Martina (Mortenson) Strand in Krustiansuund, Norway (now Oslo) January 22, 1861. In Norway people went by the name of the place where they lived or after their father's first name. Grandpa's father's name was John but he chose to go by Strand. In Norway, Dad's name was Clavin. Grandpa was a skilled carpenter and father a fisherman on the North Sea, the worlds roughest. The fishing group would be gone for two weeks at a time fishing mostly for cod and herring. The women would make bread for them and store it in a barrel. They often ate fish three times a day.

Father came to Muskegon at age 23 working in the saw mills for a $1.00 - $1.25 a day. Father was the oldest of the family, then sisters Annie Johanna, Gussiel Maria and Anna and his brother Magnus. The only relatives in America we know of are Anna, and her husband Sigvard Osho, who came to the United States on their honeymoon and settled in Mount Clemens, Michigan. Their children were John and Patsy. Their family came for Dad and Mother's golden wedding anniversary in May of 1940. John lives in Mount Clemens Michigan, and John and Betsy (Mrs. Forrest Beatty) in Florida.

Grandpa had made a chest for Dad's 18th birthday. It was a real treasure chest with beautiful finish and wrought-iron trim and handles on the front in gold English lettering

Augustinus A. Clavin January 22, 1879

Dad knew that I liked the chest, so a few years before he passed away; he said I could have it if I would take good care of it. That's the thing I miss most when our home burned in 1936.

Father said he had no trade, but it seems he could do anything that needed to be done -- farming, building, selling or mending. He kept our shoes repaired with new soles and heels. I remember how he sat by the kitchen window singing or whistling and pounding in the tacks.

Dad's first and only car was a black model T. Ford touring car, with side curtains that could be

snapped up, no heater and hand windshield wipers. Later he made it into a pickup truck to carry produce. Each year it would receive a new coat of paint. After selling the horses and getting a riding tractor, he tore down the big hay barn and built a three-stall garage with the lumber.

One morning his car was in the yard and as I backed out of the garage with mine, I bumped his a little, so when I got home from work he said, "I heard you this morning. When you touch my car or my wife you touch the apple of my eye." Dad loved mother and his car. When our home burned, his Norwegian books were gone. Later I found a large Norwegian Bible for his Father's Day gift. He was so pleased he would sit and read it for hours.

Grandpa Strand was in his 90s and Grandma in her 80s when they passed away.

2

MOTHER

Olissie Gunia Thorstenson was born in Smolen, Norway January 8, 1875 to Ole and Gertrude Thorstenson. They were the only family living on an island of one acre of land. In order to go on shore you used a boat or ran over whenever the tide came in or out.

Grandpa was a fisherman as that was the main industry in Norway. They raised sheep. The sheep were sheared, the wool

212

carded and spun into yarn. Then Grandma would weave the yarn into material to make our garments for the family. As soon as the children were five or six years old they were given knitting needles and taught to knit stockings or knit mittens for the family

The family came to America in 1885 and settled in Muskegon. Mother was 10 years old at the time. Some siblings were older and some younger. Some of the younger were born in Muskegon. When the children started school they went by three different names. The teachers were confused when they said they all have the same father, so they settled on the name of Thorstenson. Grandpa's father's name was Thorsten.

Mother didn't believe in wasting time. She required very little sleep, so she was up very early in the morning, dressed in her pretty flowered housedress, calm and ready for the day.

Laundry could be washing clothes on the washboard and hanging them out to dry or in an upstairs bedroom in winter. Water had to be carried from a pump in the front yard, but later we had water in the summer kitchen. The hand wringer was on the stand to hold the two wash tubs. White clothes were put in to boil on the wood cook stove. Ironing was necessary for most all clothing, with irons heated on the stove.

Mother loved to sew and she made most of our clothes and  her own. She would stay at the pedal machine humming and singing. Mother was always working at something -- crocheting, tatting, embroidery or quilts. We never slept on a plain pillow case - they were always beautiful with handiwork. Even though mother worked in the fields and in her many flower gardens, her handiwork was for relaxing. Mother went to work for others when she was 11 years old, so her schooling was just to the fourth grade, but she spent hours reading and she was versed in many subjects, especially in her knowledge of the Bible.

Mother had wanted to be a nurse -- and she was both in her house and in the neighborhood. In times of sickness or death she was always there to help many others.

Flowers seemed to bloom. She said you have to talk to your plants.

I guess I'll never forget the good cooking and coming home from school smelling and eating homemade raisin rye bread or warm cinnamon rolls. Dad was always proud of mother's cooking, and loved to share with company. Our round oak table in the dining room welcomed a lot of friends and family.

On grain - threshing day the men in the neighborhood came, some to work and others to visit and have a good meal. That was a busy time at our house.

In later years mother's parents moved to a farm, after several of the children were married. The farm was across the road from the school where all her family attended. Grandpa died in 1907 at the age of 59 of cancer. Grandma continued on the farm for several years with the help of some single sons. The youngest even stayed with his own family. He could keep us in stitches with his stories, and he also had a beautiful voice and loved to sing.

Mother loved people and was active in her later years as president of the ladies aid church and also of the club in the neighborhood. She taught the large adult Sunday School class at church until a few weeks before she passed away.

3

THE MARRIAGE OF AUGUST AND OLISSIE.

Father and mother met when he boarded at her home. Later he built a little house in the country and batched it for a while. Dad had fallen in love with Olissie and they were married on May 17, 1890, a special day in Norway. Shortly  after their marriage, Grandpa and Grandma Strand and Dad's youngest sister and brother came on a surprise visit. Grandpa owned two farms and he had planned to convince Dad to return to Norway and he would give him one of the farms. Of

216

course he didn't know Dad had married. They spent one year in the United States and returned to Norway.

As the family grew they move to larger places and finally purchased 80 acres of wooded land. Father cleared the land and built a log house and move there in April of 1897. Dad still worked sawmills until he was able to purchase things to start farming. Many years of farming followed. I recall having three horses -- Charlie, Molly and Dolly, besides 10 or 12 cows, pigs and chickens. Over the years, Dad had built a large barn for animals and hay. There were beautiful elm trees in the yard, so in front of the hay barn was this:

A. Anderson. Elmwood Farm

On the farm were raised acres of potatoes, corn, melons, strawberries, pickles, hay and all kinds of vegetables. On Friday – town day --Mother and Dad would go with the wagon filled with garden produce, butter and eggs. Dad was known as "cabbage King" in the neighborhood. I helped him load with beautiful cabbage to sell to the Polish and Slovak people to make into sauerkraut. They bought their needed groceries at Carl's store. Mr. Carl would always put a bag of cream candy in the sack for us children -- a real treat. One Friday I got to go with Dad and the hardware store man's daughter came out to the wagon and gave me a beautiful doll with a China head -- the only doll I ever owned.(I think that hardware man was Harry DeWitt and the young girl was likely Emma).

We had serious flooding the summer of 1925 and all crops were ruined, so dad went to work in a foundry, but continued to farm. Then on February 9, 1936, in a terrible blizzard, our home was burned to the ground. Mother went upstairs to try to put the fire out, but got out to tell Dad, who was in the barn feeding cattle.

Because of the terrible winter, I stayed at my boss' home, the Parsons. Martha and Marvin made a home for Dad and Mother until they were able to build again. At that time Larry was 18 months old so they enjoyed him. Dad was 75 years old so it was a hard experience, but they had great courage.

They sold the cows and horses, but kept one of each. Dad continued to have a large garden. Dad was a quiet man, except when he was with his own family or close friends. He would keep us in stitches with his stories. He also had a beautiful voice and loved to sing.

In Norway, the state religion was Lutheran so both mother and dad were baptized into that faith. In 1907 a group of ministers held meetings at our school house. During that time both Dad and Mother became members of the Church of God. Soon after, Dad helped build our first Church of God building in Muskegon Heights – now Woodmere Church of God. Many times visiting ministers and evangelists had dinner in our home.

Mother and Dad were married for 57 years. We had family dinners out and an open house at home for their 25th, 40th, and 50th wedding anniversaries.

Dad was in the hospital four days; he lived three more weeks and passed away at home November 9, 1948. His last words were, "Dear God, take me home." He was 87 years 10 months old.

We had family devotions after breakfast. Mother and Dad would take turns reading the Bible and leading in prayer. In those days we always knelt when we prayed, we also knelt for prayer in church.

Dad never lost his Norwegian accent. When I was away from home working or going to school, on the days that I was blue or discouraged, the thing that gave me comfort and strength, was remembering my father's voice in prayer spoken in Norwegian..

Mother wanted to spend Mother's Day with Gertrude and Joe in Milwaukee. I took her to the plane (she loved to fly) and Joe met her. While there she began having strokes and passed away June 29, 1957, age 82 years six months. Mother and Dad are buried in Norton cemetery.

Their children were Gustaf Alfred, Charlotte Lottie, Olaf Rudin, Gertrude, Morton Joseph, BabyNathan, Ruth and Martha Viola.

GUSTAV ALFRED

Gustaf Alfred -- known as Alfred

Alfred, mother, wife June, daughter June Alfreda"Blossom"

Gustaf Alfred was born March 4, 1891 at 3 lbs. 3 oz. My memories of him at home are few, since he enlisted in the Navy when I was only six years old. One thing I will never forget. On a bitter cold day I was walking home from school, one mile away. As I got close to his home, I decided to stand still and felt lost. Alfred came looking for me and carried me home. Later I learned I could have frozen to death.

When he was 17 years old a Navy recruiting ship was in town and Alfred was anxious to enlist. Dad and mother took him there. They were sure he wouldn't pass, because he had not been very well. He passed, and had to leave that same day. (1908) He was sent to Newport Naval training station in Newport, Rhode Island for training. His first leave to come home was in 1911. Martha was about 10 months old at the time. At that time our only family photo was taken. At one time his ship was to go with a fleet on a trip around the world. The folks hadn't heard from him for a long time and were very anxious, so they had the Red Cross locate him. He was in the hospital in London, and never got to go on the trip.

Another time an earthquake hit in Italy thus his ship was sent there to help build up after the ruins. He got to visit the Vatican and catacombs. World War I was on. His ship made 825 trips between the United States and France transporting men and provisions. He said that there were only two or three times that they were attacked by submarines.

On January 1, 1917, he married Gladys June Alan from Newport, Rhode Island. She would get to see him one day a month when he was on those trips. He spent 12 years in the Navy. Their only child was born May 15, 1919. They called her Blossom and she still goes by that name.

Alfred was a quiet, gentle person. He was a 50 year member of the American Veterans Legion. After retiring from the Navy he worked as a gardener at the Whitmore Estate Chateau Sur Mer near the Vanderbilt's on Ocean drive. In 1950 mother and I visited him and saw the beautiful grounds and greenhouses where he loved working at. Alfred retired at age 71 and passed away January 14, 1979 at age 87 years. Their daughter, June Alfrieda Anderson. still lives in her home in Newport Rhode Island.

It's Time to Clean the Basement Again

Editors note. We visited Blossom twice. Receiving no Christmas card two years ago I learned that she had died in Providence Rhode Island.

5

LOTTIE

Charlotte Adeline was born April 22, 1893. She was named after a good friend and neighbor of Mother's, Charlotte Cummons Stevens. Others have told me that Lottie was a beautiful little girl with long curly hair and big dark blue eyes like Dad's.

By the time I was in school, she was in high school in Muskegon Heights. She boarded with a family named Sterzik and helped with housework. They had an adopted daughter Ada, who is a few days older than me. I was invited to her seventh birthday party and to stay overnight. (My first night away from home) I slept with Lottie and Ada. During the night I cried and Mrs. Stirzik wanted to know why. I told her I had a toothache. I didn't realize I was homesick.

Lottie always had a happy disposition. Mrs. Sterzik said that even the devil couldn't make her mad. I remember Mother and Lottie doing things together like hanging wallpaper and having a lot of fun.

223

Anna Hammond was a good friend of Lottie. Ann's mother-in-law owned a boarding house so Lottie and Ann worked for her. While there Lottie met Daniel Howell. Later they were married in December, 1913, in our home.

I was 11 years old in that school. No one had told me about the wedding, but I sensed there was something going on at home, so I asked my friend Mabel Johnson, to come home with me. Lottie had made a checkerboard cake, so we each had a piece of that.
Lottie and Dan lived in Muskegon where the first three children were born. Later they moved to Grand Rapids and then finally to Hastings.

Lottie had a beautiful voice and often sang at church. As the children were older they sang with their mother in quartets, trios, etc. The new organ at a Hastings Church of God was dedicated in honor of Lottie. She suffered from cancer and other illnesses. For some time she was in a wheelchair and later in a nursing home. Lottie had experienced much sadness before she passed away. She had lost four of her children. Their first little girl Adeline at age 1 1/2 died of spinal meningitis. Ernest, was killed in Luzon, Philippines during the war. Ruth 44 years old died of cancer and left five children. Robert was young when he died, was married and left two little children.

Left to right in front Gertie, Martha, Lottie, Ruth and I think Lottie's daughter Loretta. Two sons in the back.

The Howell children were Paul, Adeline, Robert, Ruth, Faith, Ernest, Joel, Raymond, Roger, Herbert and Loretta.

GERTRUDE

Ruth and Gertie

Gertrude was born July 1, 1897, and was named after Grandma Thorstenson. She was born in the new log cabin after the folks moved on the farm. As a baby, they didn't expect her to live. Her body was weak, so she never walked until she was three years old. Mother said when they went places Dad would carry Gertie and she would carry Joseph who was two years younger. Gertie was a lot of fun. I do remember when she was in her teens, she was going to run away from home. Mother put her coat and hat on and said if anyone was going to run away – she was. I don't think Gertie ever tried it again. She liked horses and Dad let her and Joe take the team and wagon on an errand down in the field. All at once the horses started on a dead run away. Joe jumped off the wagon but Gertie hung onto the reins. As we watched them come up by the barn, Dad jumped directly between the horses and they stopped immediately. It was scary, but Dad was a brave man.

Lottie and Gertie slept together in the big front bedroom upstairs. Lottie had real long hair and at night she would make two braids for sleeping. One night in her sleep Gertie grabbed Lottie's braids, put her knees into her back thinking she was driving a horse. Of course Lottie was upset and said she was not sleeping with Gertie again. Then I got to sleep with Gertie.

I think Gertie's first job was at the Alagretti Summer Home in North Muskegon. The Alagrettis owned a chocolate company in Chicago. Mr. Alagretti died suddenly and his wife moved back to Chicago and Gertie went with her as a companion. Later she remained in Chicago and did cooking for well to do people. Gertie was an excellent cook.

Gertie liked pretty hats, so while she was working in Chicago, she saw a hat that she just had to have. Her hair was so thick that it wouldn't fit so she went to a nearby beauty shop and had them cut out enough to make a braid, and went back to get her hat.

While working in Chicago she met and married Theodore

Malmquist. He became ill and passed away when their daughter Maeruth was just seven years old.

Later Gertie married Ivan Pixley who had a funeral home in Milwaukee. The funeral parlors were on the first floor, so they lived on the second and third. There were extra

227

rooms so Gertie took care of elderly women for years. Joe lived with them and helped when they had funerals. Gertie was interested in her church and also politics. She served on several committees and campaigns and was pictured in the *Milwaukee Journal* several times.

Joe and Ivan died six months apart, but she continued caring for elderly women. After selling the funeral home and buying another house, Gertie still cared for her women.

Editor's note: Maeruth was in a hospital with tuberculosis. As a family we went to visit. This picture shows my brother Tom and me with masks on to prevent the spread of the disease I was about 9 years old.

.

Gertie had an unusual sense of humor even though she had suffered several surgeries and eye operations. She was always fun to be with. Finally she became ill and had to be in a wheelchair for several years. By then she was living with her daughter and son-in-law. They did everything for her comfort, but later she was in a nursing home where she passed away June 3, 1989. She would have been 90 years old on July 1st.

Daughter and Son in Law: Mrs. Maeruth (Richard) Dorsey
Oshkosh, WI

Maeruth and daughter Denise February 1961

Note: Maeruth died August 29, 2010

RUDIN

Olaf Rudin started the year by being born January, 1, 1895.
He was named after Uncle Olaf.
When I was about six years old and my best friend Ella was
five years old. We had walked almost the mile home from
school in a winter blizzard. We would take turns walking in
front of each other so we could breathe. We were getting near
home when Rudin came looking for us. He grabbed us by the
back of our coat collars and pushed us home. Ella's Dad
came looking for her, but Mother made her stay with me all
night.

Rudin liked to comb my blond hair when I was little and
make it fly from electricity

He had a lot of freckles and someone told him they would go
away if he would put real sour buttermilk on his face. One
night he tried it and in a short time he came downstairs and
washed it off.
He was in his teens when he had a serious illness. Mother
took care of him in their bed downstairs. He was quite short,
but they said he grew tall those weeks in bed.

 Rudin joined the Navy in 1913 at age 17 and had his training at the Great Lakes Naval Training station, Waukegan, Illinois. After training he was sent to California and Mexico. Later he spent two year in the Panama Canal Zone. Then the First World War was on so he surprised us by getting home a few days. Then back to Great Lakes for awhile before going to Brest, France, where he did the job of receiving men and provisions from the United States.

One time he and Alfred met there. On their return from France, on the ship, *Graf Waldersee*, they were nearing New York harbor at 4:00 am when their ship was rammed and sank. I believe all were rescued, but the folks didn't hear from Rudin until after they read about the tragedy in the news.

He was good at writing letters and I saved mine for years.

Once when Rudin was home on leave from the Navy, he had quite an experience. He and Dad were out on the back porch when the little neighbor girl, Helen Nelson came slowly up to them and said, "Can you come over? The bull is killing my Father." Rubin grabbed an axe and rushed across the road and found Mr. Nelson pinned against a wall between the bull's horns. He was blue in the face. Rudin asked if he could kill the bull and then hit the bull's head with the blunt end of the axe, stunning the bull and releasing Mr. Nelson – a big heavy man. I don't know about the bull, but Mr. Nelson did suffer from the experience for years.

Perhaps on the same leave, Rubin convinced Dad to shave off his mustache and beard. I remember how Martha and I cried.

It's Time to Clean the Basement Again
When Mother and Dad went to church, the usher tried to put him opposite from Mother. Even the neighbors didn't know him. Thank goodness he soon let them grow back again so he could look like our Father.

Rudin spent 8 years in the Navy and retired as Chief Petty Officer. Shortly after his returned home he married his girl friend Nettie Root from Muskegon. They went to live in Chicago where he worked for Uncle Chris who owned a cabinet shop. After learning the trade he went in business with a partner. Rudin suffered for many years with arthritis. He passed away at age 59, August 4, 1954.
They had two lovely daughters:
Mrs. Irene (Victor) Winkie Louisville, Kentucky and
Mrs. Dorothy (Robert) Sullivan Urbana, Illinois.

JOSEPH

Morton Joseph was born April 7, 1897, and named for Grandma Mortina in Norway. He had beautiful brown curly hair and when he was older he was accused of having his hair done at the beauty shop. When Joe was young, Mother's friend Mrs. Stevens wanted to adopt him. Joe and I did a lot of things together. He said if I would help him outside he would help me in the house, so we hoed corn, pulled weeds and did many farm jobs. Then he was there to help scrub our big hardwood kitchen floor on our hands and knees – and the general cleaning.

When I was ten or eleven years old Joe taught me to crochet and tat. He like to sew, thus he mended his socks and clothes. We used to ride our bikes to Fruitport 2 ½ miles to fish. We used to go berry picking, often with the horse and buggy.

One Sunday night we drove to church (at least 7 miles). Church started at 7:30 pm. It was a dark cold night. About half way home a car ran into us and ripped the left back wheel off our buggy and went right on. We fell backwards, but we were not injured. Fortunately, we had the horse that stood perfectly still. Soon another car came along and took me home while Joe and Molly walked in the cold. Dad was in bed, but got up and found Joe about a mile from home. I remember shaking all that night.

Joseph attended High School at Hackley Manual Training School in Muskegon and also worked at the Century Tailors where he learned the trade.

He fell in love with a real sweet on a girl at church named Jennie. He had her picture all over his room, even printed on a sofa pillow top. She went and married an older man, but I'm sure Joe never forgot her. He did tailoring in Chicago for several years and later in Milwaukee. There he lived with Gertrude and Ivan and helped direct whenever they had funerals.

During World War II he was drafted at age 42 and had medical training at Fitzsimmons General Hospital in Denver, Colorado. After training he was advised by his commanding officer to go back home and do defense work. Coming back he stopped in Chicago to see Rudin before returning to Milwaukee. It was a very foggy morning and their train collided with one coming from Milwaukee. Many were seriously wounded and Joe helped the doctor amputate arms and legs. Later they discovered he had worked with a crushed shoulder, so he was unable to go to work for months.

Joe had been an antique button collector since he was young and had buttons from all over the world. He was member of the National Button Collectors Club and had won several honors at their conventions.

He also kept their yard blooming with flowers from spring until fall.

Joe suffered with cancer for seven years, but was able to work until his last year. Gertrude and Ivan cared for him at home until he passed away January. 21, 1963, at age 64.

BABY NATHAN

Baby Nathan was born April 23, 1901 and lived just five months. Mother said he was the prettiest of all her babies. I'm sure it was hard for them to lose him. He died in September 1901.

10

RUTH

I, Ruth was born June 30, 1902.

My first memory was when I was four years old. Mother took me to have my picture taken. We had to go up a long stairs and the man put me up on a chair and put a black thing over his head. Just then a bell rang and I got scared and cried. Mother wanted me alone but she had to stand with me.

Just before I started school I decided to cut my tow head straight hair and climbed on a chair in front of Mother's dresser. When Mother saw it she gave me a boy cut, so when I got to school they called me a boy with dresses and that was punishment enough. I was very timid, but soon made friends, some lifelong.

When I was eleven years old I had a sunstroke while picking strawberries. I have always had to be careful of too much sun.

It's Time to Clean the Basement Again

I was too bashful to go to town to High School, but later years received a degree equivalent in Indiana. At the age of 17 I had my first job taking care of little Jewish twin boys. I enjoyed being in their home and they were very good to me. Their dad owned a men's clothing store in Muskegon Heights. Later I took care of the Shaw Walker children. In order to make more money toward going to school, I went to Chicago and did cooking in well-to-do homes.

My first real boy friend had come from Sweden two years before and worked for his uncle on the farm. He was good looking and a lot of fun.

After graduating from Anderson Bible School and Seminary in 1926 I got a job at Parson's Department Store planning to work for a month. The friend I had dated for 1 1/2 years was told by the doctor to go out west for his health, so plans changed. I guess my work had been cut out for me at home.

Editor's Note. Ruth spent some time in bed one year with what might be called depression. She had had boyfriends but never felt she could marry because she needed to take care of her parents. Rudin sent money from Chicago to help with finances and others probably helped also, but Ruth cared for her mother very faithfully. Ruth's life was family, church and work. She brought many children to Sunday School and many still remember her influence on their lives.

Aunt Ruth outside Muskegon Heights Church of God 1965.

Our church didn't have a choir, so I organized one and enjoyed working with them for many years. I also was busy teaching Sunday School with different age groups. My students were my family and church. My three nephews were a great part of my life and spent a lot of time with me when they were little. They brightened many of my days.

In 1974 I became a registered corsetiere and had the foundation department until I retired. After almost 50 years at Parson's, I retired at age 73. Then I went to work as a foster grandmother with mentally impaired children.

In April 1981 I sold the home and went into an apartment near my work. Then in July, an old friend Carl Klett called and invited me out to eat. We had known each other since I was 15 and he was 17 years old. His wife had passed away a few years earlier.

Aunt Ruth's Home ca.1975

They had two sons that I used to hold on my lap when they were small. Carl and I dated several times and we were married November 12, 1981. A small gathering of 250 people attended the wedding.

Carl had a lovely home and enjoyed his garden of flowers and vegetables.

We had five wonderful years together. I am the last of our family and now I'm blessed with two devoted sons, their loving families, and Carl's sister. Carl passed away on November 30, 1986 at age 86.

Later I moved into an apartment, but after breaking both hips, I can no longer do my own work. I am now living at the Hume Home, a comfortable care home for the elderly.

God bless and be with all.   Ruth

I enjoyed writing this and hope you will enjoy reading it too. Mother and Dad would have been proud to know all their grandchildren and their families.

11

MARTHA

Martha Viola was born November 12, 1910. She was named for Aunt Martha. No one had told me that mother was expecting a baby, so when I came downstairs one morning, Mother called me to her bedside to see my new sister. She was a pretty baby and I remember when I got to hold her for the first time. I had to sit up in a chair just right.

Martha had beautiful brown curly hair and when she was three years old she got to go with Dad and Mother to visit Rudin at Great Lakes Station.

She loved to be with Dad, and when he would plow the fields, she would follow him in the furrows all day long. One day

It's Time to Clean the Basement Again

Dad was painting our hay barn "real barn red" and Martha played near him and got her curls full of paint.

She liked to play with spiders and tomato worms, but was afraid of toads.

Martha had no neighbor children to play with so she pretended having friends. On the front open porch, she had her little table and chairs and served lunch. She was always Mrs. Jefferson. Often she played "church" seating her dolls under the big elm tree in the backyard. She did the preaching.

Martha taught our Collie dog "Rover" to play games like "hide and seek." One day the dog followed her to school and the teacher gave Martha part of her lunch to bring the dog home. After grade school she stayed in town with a family and helped with housekeeping duties so she could go to high school.

Later Martha worked at Parson's Department Store. We both worked together for several years. We had a model T. Ford and often the country roads were rough, but Martha liked to drive so we usually made it.

Next door to Parson's was a hardware store, and a young man Marvin DeWitt worked there. He would come into Parsons and soon became interested in Martha.

One Sunday afternoon he was at our door with a box of chocolates in his hand. Martha told mother to tell him she was "sick," but mother liked candy. Finally he was invited

242

in for supper. Before finishing, Martha said she had to be at her church meeting at six o'clock in the evening, so Marvin said he would take her. She had been dating another Marvin and he was at church. I often wondered why Marvin DeWitt's car had a flat tire that night. After about two years they were married and had three sons.

Marvin graduated from Muskegon Heights High School and

soon after became an employee of Highland Park Dairy,

Marvin began with the horse and wagon delivering milk and sometime later graduated to a motorized truck.

It's Time to Clean the Basement Again

Editor's note: the word pregnant was never used in our house. A woman would be "expecting" or "anticipating." I was surprised to find a picture of my mother as she was pregnant for me. You will see that below. This picture is about 70 years old

Earlier in this chapter one reads that Ruth did not know her mother was pregnant until Martha was born.

After she was alone in 1974, Martha did volunteer work at a hospital and also helped slow readers at school. She was active in her church circle and took pleasure in her sons as organists or choir members in their church while they were young. Martha did beautiful handiwork, needlepoint, quilts, etc., but her main interest was her family. For many years Martha suffered with polycethemia vera (a rare blood disease). Finally her condition turned into leukemia and she passed away July 29 1985 at age 74 years.

Sons Dr. Lawrence DeWitt deceased

Rev. Dennis J. DeWitt Holland Michigan

Thomas A. DeWitt Leesburg, Florida

12

TRANSPORTATION

The horses were great for being able to get places, with a buggy or wagon. In the winter we went with the sleigh or cutter. To keep warm we had soap stones that were put in the oven to heat, and then wrapped in a gunnysack and laid on the floor. We had a heavy robe to cover our lap.

In the 1800's an interurban track was built From Muskegon to Grand Haven, and Grand Rapids. The cars were much like train cars and they were powered by a third rail (often causing death to those that touched the third rail). In 1933 they tore out the rails and built a highway.

Of course, bicycles were used a lot. Mine was unusual. The rims and mudguards were made of bamboo so it was very light. I sometimes rode to church, but when I was 16 years old I decided I was too old to ride a bike, so I sold it.

One day we all ran out to see a bright red touring car on the road. That was my first time seeing a car. We learn that it belonged to rich people named "Judson" who owned a resort in Spring Lake.

Editor's note: we never thought of ourselves as poor, yet there was a theme in our family of servitude. My aunts all worked for "the rich" who were able to afford domestic help. Being domestic workers meant cleaning, washing and ironing and shopping for groceries.

13

MR. SHELDRUP

The folks had an old Norwegian friend, who had lost his wife. They had no children and he was not able to take care of himself. Mr. Sheldrup stayed with us for a long time. I was quite young, but I sort of remember him. I don't know what they got for taking care of him, but I do know that we had some of his antique bedroom furniture in our house that burned in 1936. His mental condition became such that he had to go to the County home.

Editor's note I do not know why this was included in the Anderson family history. One of the things stated here is that Mr. Sheldrup stayed with the family for a long time. The Anderson family housed people when their house burned or they were homeless. A cousin down the street lived with Grandma and Aunt Ruth when their house burned down.
Six children and four adults in that house made for very busy times.

ABOUT THE AUTHOR

Dennis J. DeWitt grew up in Muskegon Heights, Michigan and lives in Holland Michigan. He continues to serve Community Church of Douglas, in Douglas Michigan, part time as an Associate Pastor.

Post high school learning began at Muskegon Community College graduating in 1961. Upon graduation from Hope College in 1963 he began teaching Spanish at West Ottawa High School. In the 1960's he began graduate courses in social work and completed a Masters in School Social Work at the University of Michigan in 1974.

Completing thirty years in Education he enrolled in Western Theological Seminary graduating in 1996 with a Masters in Religious Education with focus on counseling. Later pursuing the Approved Alternate Route, a program in the Ministerial Formation Coordinating Agency (MFCA) of the Reformed Church in America, he was ordained in the Reformed Church in America in October of 2004. His wife Mary is a guest teacher in the Holland Public Schools.

Much of their family lives in the Western Michigan area. One daughter and her family live in Madison, Wisconsin, and a son and his family live in West Chester, Pennsylvania. They currently have 16 grandchildren.

Their dog Zoe is their primary ward

It's Time to Clean the Basement Again

CPSIA information can be obtained at www.ICGtesting.com
228112LV00001B/3/P

LU0005861 0320